Antiques

Antiques

HOW TO IDENTIFY, BUY, SELL, REFINISH, AND CARE FOR THEM

By Ann Kilborn Cole

Illustrated by
CYNTHIA ROCKMORE

VIRGINIA M MEYER

DAVID McKAY COMPANY, INC.
New York

Second Printing February 1958

CONTENTS

Contents

FOREWORD

FOR some years I have been conducting a weekly feature on antiques for one of our large metropolitan newspapers. When I started it there was some doubt, especially among the men on the staff, that it would "go." They did not feel it was a popular subject. That it did go over from the very beginning bore out my conviction that today everybody, including the casual reader, is antique conscious in one way or another.

I went into my new project with the idea of giving my readers a more or less over-all picture of a subject I knew and loved, one with few boundaries and many ramifications. I kept in mind that I was writing, not for the authorities in the field, not for the confirmed collectors, not for the dealers, the museum curators, or even the informed shoppers, but for the average reader whose knowledge of antiques was meager or nil but whose curiosity was acute. That I did reach such readers was evident from the correspondence that began to roll in, enlightening letters from puzzled, curious, awakened people who were avid for down-to-earth information they could understand about this hitherto esoteric subject; letters from a man who wanted to know what to do with his inherited collection of old tools; from the possessor of one piece; from an old lady who wanted to know the value of a clock brought over here by a Scots grandmother before 1850; from a woman who wanted to know how to sell a coverlet woven in 1838; a reader delighted to find out that she owned a "Landing of Lafayette" plate after reading my article on historic blue china; letters with photographs and crude sketches and almost all asking the same question: Is it antique, and how much is it worth?

But I also got letters from other people who were following my column, from collectors, curators of museums, authorities in the various fields, calling my attention to their treasures, offering information and help, and lauding my articles as interesting and accurate, all of which was most gratifying, coming from the experts. All in all my letters told me what the people wanted to know and proved that a touch of antiques, like Nature, seems to make the whole world kin.

This intense curiosity about antiques that I have been tapping has grown with leaps and bounds in the last decade. It is in tune with our times. We are not so young a country any more. We are waking up to the fact that we have an American heritage, and we are taking valiant steps to preserve it. Antiques are practically "busting out all over" America. They are no longer the playthings of millionaires. Private collections are being thrown open to the public, as witness the splendid Du Pont assemblage of antique pieces from 1640 to 1840 housed at Winterthur, Delaware. Public-spirited people of wealth have been underwriting the preservation of yesterday's relics, such as Henry Ford with his museum in Dearborn, Michigan, and the Shelburne Museum at Shelburne, Vermont, founded by Mr. and Mrs. J. Watson Webb. Small museums are springing up, like the Pennsylvania Farm Museum at Landis Valley, Pennsylvania, and the Toy Museum at Old Lyme, Connecticut. Whole towns are being restored, notably Williamsburg, Virginia; Sturbridge and Deerfield in Massachusetts; and Falsington near Penn's Manor in Pennsylvania. All of these are just a few of the many collections and museums being made available to the public. Moreover, individual houses of historical significance are being restored and furnished under various patriotic auspices like the historical societies, the Daughters of the Revolution, and the Daughters of the Confederacy. Now one can spend many profitable hours in such places as the 1704 House near West Chester, Pennsylvania, the Daniel Boone House near Reading, Pennsylvania, the Dyckman House in New York City, among many others. Old homes are being thrown open on certain days or weeks in the year like those in Natchez, Mississippi; Galena, Illinois; Wiscasset, Maine; New Castle, Delaware; or New Bern in North Carolina. Commercial concerns are collecting the antiques of their various businesses for public displays, notably the Corning Glass Museum at Corning, New York, the Hamilton Watch Collection, the Arnold Collection of Bread Trays, the Yale Antique

Lock Collection, the Home Insurance Company's exhibit of fire-fighting items in New York City, and so on. Antiques are being used as window dressing in such prosaic settings as banks and other business institutions. Antique fairs not only in the big cities but in the smallest communities attract many visitors.

People *want* to know about antiques. But how to begin?

There are hundreds of books on antiques, and at first sight it would seem that there must be enough to satisfy this growing curiosity. But my experience has convinced me that there is a need for a new kind of antique book, one for the seeker after knowledge that is not just another reference book or one channeled into any one category, a book not aimed at the antique seeker with some degree of knowledge, just a book that a reader can understand, even if he has never heard of Philip Syng, the silversmith, or seen a genuine Chelsea figurine—a handbook that will give him not only rudimentary information but the *mechanics* of recognizing, selling, buying, collecting, or just using and cherishing the old things that are likely to come into his life, a sort of bird's-eye view of the antique field as it exists today. Few of us are likely to come upon a blue dash charger of English delft or a piece of Wills pewter or a Sunflower chest outside of a museum, but how many of us know that the old gray-stone crock with the bright blue bird on it, the green lopsided bottle with an eagle on the face of it, the quaint picture "The American Homestead in Winter" that have been kicking around the family for years have a definite antique value?

And so I decided to write this book. I have not tried to add anything new to the sum of antique information or drawn any weighty conclusions. I have written what I hope is a sort of eye-opener book that will cover the subject of "antiquing" in a down-to-earth, human way. My focus has been upon the beginner. I want to tell him what he has, how to find what he wants, or dispose of what he does not want. I hope to steer him to the right books that will take up where I leave off. I want to blow away the mists from the word "antique," define it and show its value, rectifying some distorted ideas of worth and disabusing certain prejudices about antiques in the public mind. I am hoping to establish a real respect and affection for the old things that link us to our past.

Because of my dealings with the uninitiated in this big subject I think I know what you want to know when you ask: *Is it antique?* and why you ask it. Back of me is an accumulation of information and much real personal experience with antiques. I have not tried to be too technical. I can say truly that I am more interested in the personal problems of those who will read this book than in disputed earmarks of pewter or how to recognize the Dr. Wall period of Worcester china. Let the experts do the arguing. Their findings are valuable for me and for others who write the books, but they won't help you to recognize a spatterware plate or a Westward Ho! compote or an Empire chair at your neighbor's sale if you have never heard of these before.

Several things I want to establish before you read this book. I am *not* an antique dealer; my interest is purely personal, not commercial. I am considering only American antiques, which of course include many things of foreign origin imported into this country that have long been assimilated by use and familiarity. I am not going to cover such things as guns, coins, stamps, Indian artifacts, records, or musical instruments, as I feel these fields are too vast to attempt to discuss in limited space. I intend to use the word "antique" in the loose way generally accepted today by those in the business to include pieces that are often less than a hundred years old. In fact, the age of antiques today, to judge by the offerings in the shops and at antique shows, seems to have shrunk to a low of fifty years; and so, when the occasion arises, I shall include such later pieces in my chapters. After all, age is not always the most important thing in an antique. Desirability may depend upon history, rarity, or some other intrinsic value.

And so whether you have *one* piece or a houseful or none at all, I am hoping you will find answers to your questions in this book, information that will lead you on to further seeking. Many a fine collection has been started, many a home furnished, many a definitive book written from the small beginning of an inherited treasure or a whimsy bought at a country sale. But somewhere in the beginning the owner had to be shown what he had. I hope this book will do that and more for the reader.

ANN KILBORN COLE

PART I

Is It Antique?

1. WHAT IS AN ANTIQUE?

IN other words, how old is old? I wish it were easy to give a definite answer to the question. How old does something have to be to be called a genuine antique? Are all old things antiques? People are quite serious about getting the right answers to these questions. They honestly believe that all that goes into making an antique valuable is age and plenty of it. If I could say, "It must be a hundred years old at least or seventy-five years old, or even fifty years old," that would settle it for them. Then their grandmother's teapot, which must be a hundred years old, is an authentic antique to them and must consequently be worth a lot of money.

But it is not that easy. There is no hard-and-fast date for establishing antiques. True, the United States Government does set an arbitrary date of 1830 for its own purpose of collecting duty on certain imports that are not newly manufactured. Only things made before 1830 (carpets before 1700, stringed instruments before 1800) are considered antiques by Uncle Sam and thus come in duty free. This date was selected in a ruling made in 1930, and I suppose 1830 was selected because it is about the end of the period of hand-craftsmanship and the beginning of the machine age.

Among those who handle antiques as a business this date is

ignored except when they have to import their wares. A recent poll of important dealers brought out the fact that 77 per cent of them agreed that it takes a hundred years to make an antique. However, to the "trade" at large today an antique can be as young as fifty years, even less. Some antique shops play it safe and call themselves curio shops or "Yesterday Shops" so they can handle goods with less years on them without misrepresentation. Junk shops handle articles of any age with no apologies, yet here some good antiques often turn up. And many a fine antique business today began as a junk shop years ago.

The reason for this leniency about placing the age of antiques? There are several. One is that "old" antiques are getting scarcer by the minute as a result of the accelerated acquisition of them by an ever-growing, interested public, by the many new museums, restorations, business concerns, and private buyers with plenty of money to track down what they want. An antique cannot be manufactured, though many try to do it both honestly and dishonestly. It must be discovered, unearthed, ferreted out, inherited, turned over from dealer to dealer, from owner to buyer. Thus the supply is limited, and the demand grows. Antique dealing today is a sort of puss-in-the-corner business with more pieces passing through many hands than come out of hiding. As someone once said to me, "When will it come to an end?"

Well, it isn't likely to stop just like that. It will probably keep moving indefinitely. Old things are still turning up in both expected and unexpected places. Collections of years are constantly being put back on the market by the heirs of famous collectors. Sometimes even museums unload. A well-known auctioneer told me just the other day that he had been called in by a famous foundation to weed out the superfluous things and duplicates it had bought when buying was easier. But it *is* getting harder and harder for the antique dealers to stock their shops with really old and valuable pieces. However, there are still plenty of fine old things to be bought if you believe the ads in the magazines for such things as a Pilgrim ladder-back chair, a seventeenth-century salt-glazed jug, an English lantern clock, a genuine Stiegel bowl, or a Moseley tankard of American silver. But these are the big, established businesses with moneyed customers. What the average small shop deals in is apt to be of much later date, and what the average auction sale—not the fine gallery kind—disposes of is also apt to be of less importance in the scale of antiquity. And as the shops increase, and the buyers, too, things of much later vintage are being offered for sale because these are still obtainable and can be priced to fit the average pocketbook. It is estimated that at least 4,000 new dealers have come into the business in the last five years with the total for the whole country of about 12,000. It takes a lot of antiques to fill 12,000 shops.

A case in point is the tremendous interest at the moment in so-called "art glass." This is the "fancy" colored glass of the eighties, nineties, and early 1900s, the sort that graced every Victorian mantelpiece or sideboard. It is not unusual to see a single tumbler from an amberina water pitcher set priced at $18, or a signed Lutz vase for more than $100, yet as age goes they are not very old, of interest only because they fill in the picture of American glassmaking and because someone "discovered" that this Victorian "junk" had honest claims to real beauty. Perhaps they would not be so popular if there were more eighteenth-century Stiegel, Amelung, and South Jersey glass around.

Another thing that keeps antiques off the market and limits the supply is that more and more people are hanging on to what they have. They know more about antiques than they did a generation ago—just as I am hoping my readers will when they have finished this book—and they are keeping their treasures either because they have learned to appreciate them or for future profit. Because it does no harm to stockpile your antiques. It is said that many canny dealers are holding back some of their pieces for better prices in a rising market. But antiques can be as speculative as stocks on the Big Board. I have heard that some dealers overstocked with pressed glass are finding the prices dipping. However, as with the blue-chip stocks, the bottom of the market will never fall out for good antiques. It is the fads that will suffer.

To fill their shops the dealers are raiding the European markets where prices for pieces comparable to those at home are much lower. Now this practice is perfectly legitimate and does you no harm if you are not set on owning only Americana. In fact, many pieces, particularly in English and German china, are identical with the same pieces imported into our country in the 1700s and early

1800s that became naturalized over the years and are now called American. Thus I recently picked up a small Gaudy Welsh mug in a London shop that could have come out of a Pennsylvania Dutch cupboard and for which I would have paid four times as much over here.

There is one thing to be said about these "young" antiques which you see in such profusion. They will not stay young. Age will creep up on them, too, and in a few years they will season and earn a more legitimate place in the antique lineup. In a book called *Handbook of Tomorrow's Antiques* the late Carl Drepperd calls attention to many things worth saving and collecting today with future value in mind. Instead of looking backward at the antique survey, he looks ahead. Like an "unseasoned" bond with no earnings to brag about, a good piece can be "put away and forgotten" for a few years until it accumulates value.

Another reason for the popularity of these unseasoned antiques is the Victorian revival of the last few years. Suddenly everyone seemed to be discovering that the Victorian era was not all as bad as it was painted. They can look at it now with amusement or in a nostalgic mood. And so out came the Victorian pieces, some of them a hundred years old but many not more than fifty. It is a fact that Victorian will often mix better with more formal modern furnishings than American primitives. And so antiques from 1860 to 1900 are accepted in the very best circles.

But, as I have intimated, more goes into the making of an antique than mere age. Often, looking over the shelves or poking through the barns of the dealers, I am struck with the thought, "Why were some of these things saved at all?" because many of them are not appealing, to say the least, and are often undeniably ugly. Just because something is old is no guarantee that it is in good taste. There was bad taste years ago as there is now. Of course much depends upon the individual likes of the owner or buyer. Beauty, after all, lies in the eye of the beholder. However, if you are a student or a collector of Americana, beauty may be of no consideration. To a true collector I can believe that nothing is ugly if it is rare or storied or fills in the links of the chain. To him the chase is often more important than what it leads to.

And so aside from beauty it would seem that there are other factors that enter into making an antique worth holding or buying. Rarity is an important one. Take Tucker china, for instance, made for only a short period in Philadelphia up to 1838, when the firm succumbed financially. Not too much could have been made in the decade of operation, and while it is a beautiful example of the potter's art, imitating as it did the best French imports of the period, it is not unrivaled by any means. Yet it is valuable because not too much of it survives and also because it represents one of the few American attempts at early china making. So added to a fairly ripe age of 120 to 130 years are beauty, rarity, and historical significance. A true antique.

The question is often asked, when does a restored piece cease to be an antique? In other words, can it still be called an antique if new wood or patches or hardware have been added? I have talked to various dealers and restorers about this. The opinion seems to be that if 60 per cent of the original piece has been left in the restoring it can still be called an antique. However, this is not a hard-and-fast rule. The older and rarer a piece the more leeway can be given to new additions and substitutions in order to bring it back to some semblance of what it originally was, on the principle that it is better to save even part of a dilapidated old piece than to let it go completely.

Honest dealers will usually acknowledge any restoration. They will say, "The bracket feet are new. When we got it someone had put on ball feet which weren't right for the period." Or, "Only ten of the sixteen brasses are old on that chest." Or, "The base of that tavern table is old but the top was newly made from old wood." Naturally the more restoration and addition of new material the less valuable the piece, but even so I—and I'm sure many more like me—would prefer an old piece authentically brought back to usefulness, even if less than the 60 per cent were there to begin with, than an entirely new reproduction. I feel sure, too, that many a piece sold as antique has seen enough mending over the years to jeopardize this 60-per-cent rule. Restoration and renovation have gone on for a very long time.

And except for its value in dollars, what does it matter? I have a little Staffordshire mantel figure, an old market woman, that I dearly love. A long time ago she must have had a smashup, for the base has been crudely filled with cement and painted over. She is certainly not proof, or mint, as they say. But she's good enough to occupy an important place on my mantel. I didn't pay much for her, and I don't expect to sell her. She's antique enough for me.

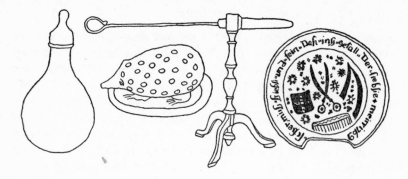

2. WHAT IS IT?

Dear Miss Cole,

I have in my possession an old platter which I know is old because it belonged to my father's aunt. It's blue and has a fancy edge and some kind of a foreign scene in the center. Is it of any value? And how can I sell it?

HERE is a typical letter from a reader who in all good faith believes that I can identify and appraise her platter from such a meager description. There are many like her, all of whom I must disappoint when I say I cannot possibly tell what they have without better information or without seeing the piece—perhaps not even then. Because the curious thing—and also the most interesting—about antiques is that something new is always turning up to stump the experts just about the time when they think they have a whole category covered and classified. So to my dear readers I explain that what might seem to be on brief description a valuable piece of Canton, perhaps even a Minton willow, a Clews historic blue, or a Mason ironstone could be merely a leftover from a dinner set sold by Homer Laughlin or Montgomery Ward.

Identifying an antique piece of furniture, glass, china, or silver takes a lot of doing and often much research. But even worse is the naming of some mysterious piece that has no counterpart in any category. Often your guess is as good as mine though here the historians with more knowledge of the habits and customs of bygone

9

times may come to the rescue. I remember when I first saw a Pennsylvania sgraffito plate with a large hunk cut from the rim—not broken, but made that way. It was some time until I learned that it was a barber's dish, made so that it could be held under the chin to hold the lather. It also took a bit of conjecturing until I was able to place the ornate iron vase in a shop as a "humidifier" from an old parlor stove. A basalt porcupine with holes in his back was an old crocus or bulb jar so a dealer had to tell me, though I might have guessed it. I did guess right on a beautiful glass pyramid among a collection of varicolored paperweights—a wig stand. Did you ever see a "hurdy-gurdy"—not the street kind? I had to have that named for me and it sent me scurrying to the library to find that in the Pennsylvania Dutch country a descendant of a very old musical instrument used by the beggars of Europe in the tenth century could exist. Would you recognize a horse net, a silver medicine sipper, or a pitcher bib?

This kind of identification is work, but fascinating. However, the authority who knows his or her subject can usually hit it on the nose without too much delving.

But how is the average owner of one or several or a houseful of old things going to get this professional advice? Ah, there is the question. It isn't something you can do in a hurry, but if you really want to know what you have inherited, to find out what that barrel of china and glass left over from the old homestead might contain, if you suspect you have a treasure in that old doll or faded fire screen, it is worth taking the trouble to find out. Particularly is this true if you are sure you do not want to use it or keep it for sentimental reasons and are willing to turn it into cash. Before you can sell your antiques you should know what they are *worth* (Chapter 3), and to establish that you must first know exactly what they *are*. To you an old smudgy blue plate might be just a piece of china that "ran" in the making, whereas it could be a valuable piece of Flow Blue Staffordshire and worth possibly $35 or $40. On the other hand, that willow plate used in the family for years and slightly crackled might be only part of an American-made willow set bought at the five-and-ten and worth nothing.

So it comes back to finding the right answer either by yourself or with help. Don't depend too much on what the family tells about it.

Word-of-mouth history can be strangely garbled over the years, though it does help. What is more important are any family papers that mention it, letters, journals, bills, accounts, etc. If you know the approximate time the family acquired it you have taken a good first step. Now there are all kinds of antique books on the market to help you in your search. Many of them have pictures and drawings and diagrams just for this purpose of identification. For your reference I have included a bibliography at the end of this book. Particularly is this true of furniture, china, and glass. A little glass and much china are marked—another help, for there are a number of books containing china marks of all countries. There are also books containing silver marks and pewter touch marks. If you have a marked piece, it won't be too hard to trace if it is at all important.

"But I don't want to buy a lot of books just to find out about a few pieces," you will say. Of course you don't. The first step is to see what your local library has on its shelves. Libraries are stocking many more antique books these days because people are asking for them. If you live near a large city, a day spent in the main library will probably give you all the information you need. Don't hesitate to ask for help. Some historical societies have libraries which are of great help. Or perhaps your local library will order books for you from the state library if it has an extension service. But of course you should know what books you want. Many antique dealers have extensive libraries of their own, and if you know one well enough he or she might let you consult it.

"But suppose I do want to buy a few books, how do I find them? My bookstore doesn't carry them, or only a few expensive ones. They say they can't find some on my list," someone is sure to say. I can see how that can happen. Many books on antiques have been privately printed, or put out by small firms that specialize in such items. I shall put at the end of this chapter some of the sources from which you can order many of the books I list, at any rate those still in print. For some of the old standbys that are out of print you will have to rely upon the libraries or the secondhand bookshops. These are other fine sources for picking up books on antiques. After all, a good informative book does not go out of style.

Then there are the magazines that are concerned with antiques wholly or in part. I shall list them also. Both the ads and the articles are very helpful and they are interesting even if you don't possess many antiques. If you have access to these in your library, you can do a lot of research. Ask the librarian to help you look up your topic either in the index which several of them put out or in the *Periodical Index,* because many other magazines publish articles on antiques, too. Of course for such study you have to have some idea of what you possess. You can't start from scratch in this way very well.

But you can make the rounds of the antique shops in your neighborhood. There are few localities that don't have at least one good shop these days. Just browse around until you see something that looks like what you have and then find out what it is. Of course this is going to take time, but what's the hurry? That platter has been on the top shelf of the kitchen cupboard for a good many years already. What will another few months matter? Certainly it will not depreciate with time. And in the meantime you are learning new things and having fun. It gives you a wonderful excuse for talking to interesting people. It broadens your whole scope of interests. You may not even find out exactly what that platter is, but the search will prove an open sesame to a whole new life for you.

After the shops, visit the antique shows and fairs. Here you can cover a lot of ground in a morning or afternoon—and perhaps even spot the duplicate of your platter.

So much you can do for yourself, but there are people who can help you if you ask for aid in identifying an antique. When you visit the shops, talk to the dealers. Most of them will lend an ear if you catch them in an idle moment. But do not buttonhole a shopkeeper at a busy time when he might otherwise be making a sale. That is a thoughtless discourtesy and foolhardy to say the least. You won't learn much that way. Not that every antique dealer is omniscient by any means, but I am continually surprised at how much they do know and how quickly they accumulate their knowledge. Of course there are dealers and dealers. One successful husband-and-wife pair I know who specialize in the fine stuff keep studying all the time. They have a case of reference books that would shame most libraries. To them the business is more than a dollar-and-cents affair. I know others like them.

On the other hand, I recently read a story told by Alice Hulett

Metz in one of her articles on old glass in *The Antiques Journal*. It seems when a customer asked for Sandwich glass the dealer pointed to a block-patterned pressed-glass piece, and when challenged, remarked, "But of course it's Sandwich. See all the little square sandwiches in the pattern?" It's hard to think anyone could be that stupid, but maybe the dealer figured he had a stupid customer.

Other sources of help you can get free are the museums and the historical societies. Large museums usually have a department that will identify your antique pieces, though they will not evaluate them. As far as the smaller institutions go that are not supported by public funds I would imagine it might be a matter of the individual curator's good nature or good will, or whether the museum can afford to keep an authority on the staff with time to give to this work. That you would have to find out. But whatever you do, don't go asking questions with only half the story. If possible, take your piece with you. This is the shortest cut to identification, as often much depends upon the "feel" of the piece, the weight, texture, depth of color, age of wood, variations in pattern, and so on—details that no description or even a photograph could catch. A dealer once told me—I give it to you for what it is worth—that she could detect a bogus dolphin candlestick by the feel of it. In an old piece there will be a difference in temperature between the dolphin and the top when held with both hands. Experts on milk glass hold a piece up to the light to find the "oyster" in the bottom, the spot where the glass in congealing made a sort of swirl. I have been told that this is not a sure-fire test because some old pieces do not show it and some new ones do. However, the point I am making is that in both cases these pieces had to be *handled*.

If you can't carry your piece with you, take a picture of it. It's a big help. If it is glass, you can take rubbings by laying a piece of thin paper over the glass and rubbing it with a soft pencil. This brings out the design. You can do the same with silver hallmarks or pewter touch marks. Or you can make a rough sketch of it to record the general shape and measurements. Look for and jot down the markings, if any. On furniture you may find mysterious names or dates burned on, scratched, or painted. These may not establish the origin of the piece but will be some guide to its history, an owner if not the maker, or a date when it was inherited. On the back of a

cherry corner cupboard that belonged to my grandfather I discovered, when it was moved from the corner where it had stood for
years, that there was a chalk-marked date of 1812 which is about the
date I would have guessed. Who put it there or why it had never
been rubbed off I don't know, but someone had labeled it, and I
was delighted with the information. Be careful not to confuse
patent numbers with dates. A friend of mine declared for years she
had a chair from 1786 which was actually made at least a hundred
years later in the Victorian era and had a patent label on it. Of
course if you should find a genuine old label, you are in luck. Even
the label, if old enough, will be valuable.

An old furniture label.

Appraisers—of which more later in the next chapter—will, of
course, identify as well as evaluate for a fee. Unless you want to sell
or at least establish value for insurance purposes this is an expensive
way of finding out what the article is.

You can also ask the help of those who edit antique columns in
magazines or newspapers. Some of these columns invite queries and
hire experts to answer them. Don't be too greedy. I know of one
magazine that had to limit the questions to *one* item because their
service was being abused. And if you do ask for this information, be
as definite as you can—as I have suggested before. And *do* send a
stamped and self-addressed envelope for reply even if you are not
requested to do so. The editor will feel more kindly toward you
and will turn handsprings to answer your question.

One more suggestion for securing knowledge about your antiques.
Join a club. There are many groups gathered and held together by

their common interest in antiques. Some are local and some are national. The Questers, which began in a small way in Pennsylvania, is now a well-known national group with chapters all over the country. Another name you meet is the Antiquists. There are also many specialized groups having to do with antique collecting, like the Association of Paperweight Collectors, the Button Society, Music Box Society, Wedgwood Society, and so on. It is estimated that there are about a hundred of such organizations. A letter to one of the antique magazines or a local antique dealer will probably give you information about groups in your area.

Magazines

Antiques, 601 Fifth Avenue, New York, New York

Spinning Wheel, Taneytown, Maryland

The Antiques Journal, Westfield, New York

Hobbies, 1006 S. Michigan Ave., Chicago, Illinois

Yankee, Dublin, New Hampshire

American Heritage, 551 Fifth Avenue, New York 17, New York

The Antique Collector, 16 Strutton Ground, Victoria St., London S.W.1, England

Book Sources

Antiques Publications, Ladiesburg, Maryland (Send $1.00 for their catalogue.)

Century House, Watkins Glen, New York

The Antique Journal Bookshop, Westfield, New York

Warman Publishing Co., 8 Frankhoover St., Uniontown, Pennsylvania

The Antiques Book Society, 123 Middle Neck Road, Great Neck, New York (monthly membership)

The Bookshop of James J. Kane, 135 East Thirty-fourth St., New York City (old and new books)

Arnold N. Johnson, Petersham, Massachusetts (old books)

Goodspeed Bookshop, Boston, Massachusetts (rare books)

The Book Barn, Lenape Rd., West Chester, Pennsylvania (old books and back copies of *Antiques*)

Ruth Webb Lee, Framingham, Massachusetts (handles all her own books and will autograph them)

Leary's Book Store, 9th and Market Sts., Philadelphia, Pennsylvania (old books and new)

The World Publishing Co., Cleveland (for series of American Arts Library of $1.00 books)

Mentor Books. (The New American Library of World Literature), 501 Madison Ave., New York (for *How to Know American Antiques* by Alice Winchester, paperback)

Lightner Publishing Co., 1006 S. Michigan Ave., Chicago, Illinois

Suggestions

A Library of Ceramic History is maintained by the Franciscan Order at the Franciscan Library of Ceramics, 45 East Fifty-first St., New York City, for the use of any researcher.

Get yourself on the mailing list of several of the big "book remainder" firms which send out lists of bargains occasionally.

Publishers Central Bureau, 419 Fourth Ave., New York City

Brentano's, 586 Fifth Ave., New York City

Marboro Books, 222 Fourth Ave., New York City

3. HOW MUCH IS IT WORTH?

BEFORE you can know what an antique is worth you must know what it is. In the previous chapter we have discussed ways and means of finding out what you have. Most of the agencies for *identifying* antiques will go no further—unless they want to buy it. Even a dealer will be cautious about putting a price on your piece. He is more apt to say, "What do you want for it?" and if you don't know the value of it you are stumped. He may not know either, or his question could be just a canny way of making you come out with a low asking price and putting the responsibility on you if it turns out a steal for him. However, if all the stories that dealers tell are true, this does not happen often any more. Sellers are far more apt to have an exaggerated idea of what their antiques are worth.

To the uninitiated the word "antique" is written in dollar marks. If a thing is old, it must be worth a lot of money. They have heard fantastic stories to substantiate this. For instance, when an iron mechanical bank called Columbine and Harlequin was sold at a famous sale for $3,000, everyone with an old iron bank began to dream dreams of opulence, whereas many good banks can be bought for $25. Once I wrote about a glass paperweight no larger than a quarter that was worth $2,500. Everyone who read my article went running to the dealer who had sold it to the collector with all their old paperweights. Not one was worth more than $5. So, a warning! Don't get illusions about the value of your antiques until an expert has appraised them. On the other hand, don't give them away for a pittance. Don't stop at one offer. Investigate. And remember that the antique that sells for an astronomical price has probably passed through many hands which have each taken a profit from it.

There is no doubt, however, that today antique values have risen considerably and for many reasons. First, there are more buyers. The public, as I have pointed out, has become more aware of antiques and their values. This began in the World War II years when new things were hard to get and people went to the antique shops and came out with more for their money than if they had purchased shoddy new pieces. Second, money is easy. Antiques are participating in the wave of economic prosperity. Third, there are fewer antiques to be sold. The market is shrinking. Museums and collectors have cleaned up much of the finer and older things. When a collection is broken up and put on sale it doesn't take long for it to be absorbed. Remote sections of the country are being opened up with good roads, and old houses with old pieces no longer lurk in the backwoods undiscovered. Again people are holding on to what they have, even the younger people, if for no other reason than that they realize that a good antique, like the chorus girl's diamonds, is money in the bank for times of stress. Of course prices can slip in any business recession when people have to unload their assets, but for a long pull they are a fine investment—if you have not paid too much for them in the first place.

It is easy to pay too much for certain things that are fads. Every year various articles spring up that everyone wants because everyone else is collecting them. A few years ago, for instance, it was ruffled-glass bride's baskets. Old tin pieces brought big prices because everyone was painting tin, and right now it is calendar plates. A few years ago you could buy a calendar plate if you wanted it for fifty cents or $1. Now I see them advertised for as much as $6. They aren't especially pretty. I can't see them holding up in the antique market indefinitely. Or take pressed glass. Patterns come and go in popularity but chiefly because of availability. Lion Glass, Westward Ho! Daisy and Button, Bellflower, Rose in Snow, and Roman Rosette, were being grabbed up by everyone when the pressed-glass furore started some years back, with prices rising from about thirty-five cents for a goblet that brings $6 to $10 today. It was a "fad" that has held up fairly well because women still collect pressed glass and are still filling out their collections, but new patterns are taking on more importance, such as Diamond Band, Late Thistle, Block and Fan, Cottage, Palmette, Bridle Rosette, and so on, and their prices will rise as the fad gains momentum. I am not belittling the collecting of good pressed glass, but I am trying to point out that fads "up" prices more than real value. However, it often happens that the fads of today are the respectable antiques of tomorrow. It is something to think about if you decide to follow the crowd to the antique shops. According to the ads, pattern glass is still selling for good prices, but I have heard rumors that in some sections it has

Once worth five cents, coffee mills such as this Victorian one now sell for over five dollars.

slumped. Maybe the "girls" are stocked up or tired of it or have gone on to the newer "art" glass. Or what is more likely, it is suffering in competition with imports and reproductions. But it is not a big dip to worry about.

There are other ways in which you can get stuck, and the chief one is in not knowing enough about what you are selling or buying. But in general this fact is true at the moment: if you are buying you will pay high prices, and if you are selling you should be getting more than you would have got last year and perhaps not so much as you might get next year.

But we still have not answered the question: How are you going to know what to ask or what to take for what you have? Now even in the antique business, where there never was or could be a fair trade ruling to equalize prices, there are certain price ranges that do not vary too much. Of course all prices are influenced by the supply, on how much and how many people want it, by the condition of the pieces, and by locality (local demand). In resort areas in the "season" prices will soar. Vacation money is easy, people have more time to shop. They see different things and they want to bring something home with them. The best time to buy in such places is just before the season opens, when the dealers need money to replenish their stocks, or when the season closes and they are glad to get rid of stock that they might have to hold over for the next season and thus tie up their money for another year. In prosperous areas prices will be higher than in backwoods sections. Prices in the East are said to be lower than on the West Coast, as the tide of antique interest moves westward. Western states have their own antiques, it is true, but when they want the early Americana such as is sold in the East, they must pay for it. All that did not go West in the covered wagons or around the Cape has to be imported from eastern dealers often by the truckful. This brings in a middleman and helps to boost the prices. Right now I would say that the Middle West is a highly lucrative area for the dealer both for buying and selling, because it has "waked up" more recently to the great attraction of antiques.

But, generally speaking, in any one locality you will find dealers' prices fairly uniform. They watch each other's stock closely. So if you have something to sell, the easiest way to determine its worth (in the market, not to you) is to make the rounds of the shops and see what they are asking for the same thing or something similar. Of course you must remember you will not get the dealers' selling price. You must be resigned to taking a third or a half less. Some dealers figure their markup on the time they expect to hold the piece. If they have a customer in the market for what you have to sell, they may be open to bargaining, and will give you more because of the quick turnover.

Another and perhaps easier way to learn about antique prices is to go to an antique show. At a show you can cover twenty, thirty, or more dealers in one day. Ask questions. Carry your piece with you, or a picture of it. Dealers do a lot of buying at shows, particularly from each other. Even if one dealer is not in the market for what you have he may tell you who is or give you an idea of what it is worth. You'll find them surprisingly co-operative.

You shouldn't have trouble finding an antique show in your locality no matter where you live. This institution is springing up all over the country, spreading to the smallest towns and communities. They are listed in the antique magazines. *Antiques* carries a calendar of shows, listing the dates for several months ahead and for the whole country. So does *Spinning Wheel. The Antiques Journal* lists some of the more important shows and auctions. Watch your local paper for ads. In the current issue of one magazine I have counted seventy-five shows for the late fall and winter months from Tulsa, Oklahoma, to Sarasota, Florida. They are promoted by associations of antique dealers, professional organizers, women's clubs, and church groups. They are good business, although some dealers pass them up, particularly those who rely on certain moneyed, tried-and-true clientele. Others say they make no money but it is good publicity for good shows draw people from near and far. Some towns even have two shows sponsored by different groups, a spring show and a fall show. At this writing New York has three, the Fall International Antiques Exposition held now in the new Coliseum, and a spring show at the Armory at Thirty-fourth Street. Another fall show for charity is given at the 69th Regiment Armory at Lexington Avenue and Twenty-sixth Street.

Another way to get an idea of values is to read the ads in the antique magazines. Do it diligently, and after a few copies you will be surprised at how much you have learned. Going to antique sales is another way to absorb prices and values. You may never raise your voice in a bid, but just sitting in on a big gallery sale in a large city is an experience, especially if you buy a catalogue and jot down the prices the various items bring. It will be an eye opener. Smaller sales vary according to the crowds they attract, to the weather, and the date, which might be competing with some other important local event. A bunch of acquisitive buyers with plenty of money can upset the price level considerably. But all in all they are fairly representative of what the public will pay. A captain's chair in the rough may bring $15 at one sale (about the price you would pay for it in a shop) or it might go to $18 or $20 to a buyer not familiar with the market. Or if the day is stormy and the attendance lean, you might get it for $12 against a dealer who knows what it will bring in his shop. But at least you get the range, and one day if you do pick up an unfinished captain's chair in fair condition for $10 you know you have a bargain. Many of my dealer friends do not go to sales any more because they say the prices are too high for them. After all, they are competing against individuals who do not have to resell what they buy for a profit. On the other hand, some of my friends say they cannot compete with the dealers who may have a good-paying clientele to unload on. One expects to get things cheaper at a sale but it does not always work out that way.

A frequenter of sales learns many things even if he buys nothing. He finds out that a crack, a nick, or heat or age craze, or a missing part immediately lowers the value. The bidding dealers may buy in such things but they know that only perfect pieces will bring the big prices. (There is no percentage scale to determine how much a crack or chip detracts from the value. It just depends upon who wants it, and how much.) He finds out that matching pairs of many things bring *more* than twice what a single piece would bring. A good auctioneer will try not to break up a set, but if the bidding is sluggish he may have to. Sometimes in this case the first bidder gets the bargain, the price moving up when the other matching pieces are put up and the competition wakes up and gets hot. Sometimes it works the other way when the early bidders have had their choice. I remember once at a sale in Maine I lost my bid on a pair of early rush-bottomed pine chairs. The buyer decided to take only one. The auctioneer asked me if I would like the other one at the same price and I said yes. But when I claimed it, I found that the rush in my chair was artificial while the other was real rush. However, I still think I got a good buy, but if I had been more alert I would have upped my bid in the first place and had first choice of the pair.

You will pick up a lot of odd information at sales just listening and watching, things like evaluating a Jenny Lind bottle by whether it has a tree on the reverse side or not—the tree bottle is rarer—or determining the authenticity of a Bennington hound-handled pitcher by measuring the space between the head and the paws with a small finger. If it slips through and if the dog wears a chain and if the underpart of the body is neither flattened nor too well rounded, you probably have a genuine piece. You find out that an arrow-back plank chair brings more than a half-spindle chair and that a bent arrow-back brings more yet. Just by listening you'll find out why the old stone jug with a handle that connects the neck and the bottle brings more than the jug with the handle applied only to the body—the first is older. You'll discover why a pile of old plates sold for such a high price—there was a showy flowered one in the middle which was Gaudy Dutch, and why a few minutes later another plate almost the same brought much less—it was Gaudy Welsh recognizable by its luster banding.

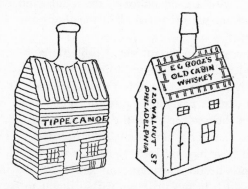

These two log-cabin bottles look similar but are dollars apart in value.

There are books of retail price lists published on various groups of antiques. I have listed a few in the bibliography. You will find the ads for such price guides in the various antique magazines. They are revised from time to time to keep step with the market, and while they do not and cannot give *exact* values—impossible considering that so many factors enter into the determination of the price asked for any antique—they do give you an idea of what your piece or pieces might bring at retail either to yourself selling to a private buyer or to a dealer selling to the general market. I've heard criticism that some of these books are misleading, but I still think they are valuable if they are not accepted as gospel truth, only as indications of a price range. For instance, have you any real idea what that old woven coverlet of yours should bring *retail?* It has a date, 1840. It's in good condition. You look it up in a price guide. Two coverlets are recorded there at $30 each, which is the usual market price. A worn coverlet will bring less, a particularly fine one in a rare pattern or very early will bring more. But at least you have an idea, and you won't be inclined to sell it for $5. Or take a list of prices for Currier and Ives prints and other old lithographs of the 1800s. Now there are all kinds of modifying factors when you sell a print—age marks, watermarks, size, cut-down borders, etc.—which might bring your Currier and Ives print down to a much lower value, so instead of getting $150 for your fox-hunting picture you might have to take $50 from a collector. You have to learn to use such lists with a good ounce of discretion, and remember the prices quoted are the prices asked in the shops, not what a dealer will give you.

And now we come to the subject of professional appraisers. There are firms and individuals whose business it is to appraise antiques. Not too many will do it on a small scale. Generally it does not pay them and it doesn't pay you to put out money for a small evaluation. Some of them advertise in the antique magazines. I have seen ads, however, that set a minimum of $5 per item or related group which might bear looking into. Generally the appraisers are more interested in collections, estates, and acting for the big insurance companies, which brings up a point that ought to be considered—insurance. If you have a sizable collection of antiques, it needs special insurance consideration. It doesn't take long to run up a value of several thousand dollars if you've been collecting for any length of time or if you have been left a few good pieces. You'll surprise yourself when you begin to take an inventory of what you have. I was when I went through my house a few years ago for a new policy. Not that I had paid half what it totaled, but the replacement value of the moment brought it up to an astounding figure—for me. Here is where you can use an appraiser. Fortunately I was familiar enough with the market to do it for myself. What your insurance agent will try to sell you now is a comprehensive policy that covers fire, theft, water, smoke, vandalism, windstorm, and other hazards. He will probably write into it a "fine arts" clause in which the most valuable of your possessions are listed with their values. If something happens, it will save you a lot of arguing and proving. Of course values change from year to year and it is well to keep this in mind and revise your policy often.

Some dealers have an appraising service which they charge for. It saves them from being annoyed by people who would be no asset to their business and it gives them a lucrative side line. The point to watch here, of course, is whether they are appraising with their own advantage in mind in case you want to sell. Better check first with such an organization as the Appraisers Association of America, 47 West Fifty-seventh St., New York City, to see if such a dealer is in good standing, or if they can recommend a good appraiser in your area. If you do approach a dealer for information about value, it might be a courteous thing to ask if there is a fee for this service. I know my articles have unleashed many queries on the dealers and I hope it has brought business to those who have been so good to me. However, when a dealer does give you such information gratis, remember it is a favor and he should not be imposed upon.

Don't count upon the museums to set a price on your antiques. They refuse to put themselves out on such a limb, and rightly. And don't ask anyone, your favorite columnist or editor for instance, to set a value on something he has not seen. It won't work. I can tell you a funny story on myself right here about a wild-goose chase that I made with a friend of mine last year. A correspondent told me she had some Currier and Ives prints she would sell, named the size, even the titles. They sounded good, and my friend who was interested in prints would have bought them sight unseen if the price had been right. I suggested looking at them first, so we set off on a trip up country looking for the little village where the correspondent lived. We found it and we found her, a smiling, courteous country storekeeper. But when she brought out the prints they were nothing, just a batch of cheap chromos in cheap modern frames. When I asked her how she got the idea they were Currier and Ives prints she said a social worker who had been staying in the vicinity for a time had told her so, and also that they were valuable. She hadn't been trying to cheat, she just didn't know. But my friend would have been badly stung if she'd bought them by mail.

Another time a friend of mine heard of a Bennington Coachman bottle, a very desirable item, which was for sale. She made a reasonable offer by mail. But when the bottle appeared there were two obvious chips in it which the owner thought "wouldn't matter." Because my friend wasn't planning to resell the bottle, the chips did not make too much difference, but she dropped her bid and got the bottle for much less. The owner was happy because it was still more than a dealer had offered her and my friend was happy that she had not paid first and looked afterward.

But all this takes time, you say. It does. You can't sit home and expect enlightenment to descend upon you from the sky. You can't expect other people to do all the work of pricing for you. You must be prepared to go and find out for yourself. And don't expect too much from your friends or depend too much on idle gossip. You'll hear things like this: "Why, I know someone who sold a china teapot the other day for $50. I wouldn't take a cent less for that one you have." But the first teapot may have been Spatterware and yours might be late American ironstone.

So what do you do? You make up your mind either to find out for yourself by one of the methods I have suggested or you figure it isn't worth the trouble, and when a dishonest dealer comes calling and offers you $1 for the old blue glass butterdish you let him have it. Watch the dealers whom you don't know who come to your house uninvited. Some may be honest "spotters" for dealers, but many are not. If they make you an offer, say you will think about it and ask for their name and address, and keep an eye on them while you talk to them. Small things fit easily in overcoat pockets. Don't let them gather up a lot of "junk" and offer you a flat price for it. Twenty-five dollars might seem like a lot in your hot little hand, but if you are like a member of my family it may mean the loss of a pair of bisque figurines, a miniature amber hobnail tea set, two fine celery vases, a lot of cut glass, three bottles including a log-cabin Booz bottle, and a Bennington Toby jug, not to mention the odds and ends of a Haviland dinner set.

There is one value I have not discussed. What does your old piece mean to *you?* Has it associations? Do you have to sell it? If it will give someone else pleasure, why not you? Are a few dollars enough for what you can get out of it? I know people are curious to know the value of what they possess. They prize an article more if they know it is worth more. But unless there is financial need, why worry? Enjoy your antique for itself. Or if you don't want it, remember there are others who might. Pass it on. Antiques make fine gifts for the right people. Yes, there are values in antiques besides the dollar mark, values that are more easily measured.

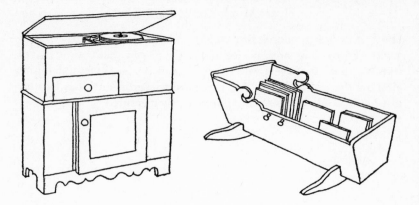

4. WHAT TO DO WITH IT

I AM assuming you have discovered that you own some antiques. You have found out what they are and you have a fairly good idea of what they may be worth. So now what are you planning to do with them? Will you sell them or keep them?

Let's say you have decided to sell and get some money out of that old "trash" you've uncovered in the attic or the cellar. It means nothing to you. Any family association has long been lost. Your children call the stuff old-fashioned. Or if it has family history you feel you have no heirs who would appreciate it. That old slope-front desk might be something from the antiquarian viewpoint but it would cost a lot to have it fixed up. Moreover, you have a desk that fits your modern *décor*. And Betty, who is twelve and about to take music lessons, does need a piano. So why not take the $500 you have been offered for it and buy a new spinet piano for Betty?

Now perhaps I don't agree with you, but you have a right to do the thing you think best. In this case a bona-fide offer has been made by a dealer who has had his eye on that desk for some time and has come up from $300, his first bid, to $500. That desk must be worth quite a bit. You can play him along because he may be nowhere near the top yet. However, if you know exactly what you have, its age, history, etc., it might pay you to shop around and see if you can find someone who'll offer more. Or you can sell it to a private buyer. You may do better, you may not. Remember that the dealers know the big buyers in the market for certain pieces and you do not. But you can advertise it. In the case of a piece as valuable as this it would most certainly pay to risk a few dollars on an ad either in your local paper or in one of the antique magazines. Now that you know what you have to sell, and with the $500 offer to go on, you could act on your own.

But all antique selling is not that easy. The obvious and easiest way to dispose of your antiques, especially if you have only a few pieces, is through a dealer. As I have said before in this book you must be prepared to take a lot less, a third, a half, or maybe even less, of what it will eventually sell for. That's why it is so necessary for you to know what the current market price is. Now even the most honest dealer could not stay in business long if he were soft-hearted enough to give big prices for what he buys. This is a hard business. It makes sharp people. The dealer who knows his business has a lot of things to consider. Can he spare the cash at the moment to buy anything? Winter and bad roads are ahead. Business may slump. He wants to keep some cash reserve for a big sale that is coming up, and so on. He can always get plenty of good coverlets. However, if he can get yours cheap enough he might risk taking on another. Yours is a rather nice one, dated and in good condition. So he tries you out with a low offer—and he is *not* trying to gyp you. If you don't like his price you don't have to take it. He won't care. But if you find another dealer who offers you more, don't go around saying the first one is a pirate and a robber. While I know there are plenty of close dealers in this business, I know, too, that stories like this are told about almost everyone in the business who buys from the public.

Some dealers will not buy this way at all. They prefer to go after what they need or want. If they don't know you, they run the risk of buying stolen property or even fakes. So they play safe.

I've heard it said so often—I've said it myself—"How is it when you try to sell an antique you get so little for it, yet when you go to buy the same thing you pay through the nose?" It's very true. There is usually a big spread between the buying and selling price on antiques, probably more than in most commodities. But this spread varies. You might be lucky enough to strike a dealer at the time when he *needs* exactly what you have for a waiting customer, and because he does not have to hold the piece but can make a quick turnover and please a good customer he'll give you a better than usual price. Or his stock may be low and he is ready to buy almost anything to fill up his shop. And so I always advise my readers never to take the first offer, not because I think the first dealer will necessarily prove unfair but because other dealers might be in a better position to make the purchase more interesting.

You may ask, "But why does a dealer have to do this? It isn't costing him anything to hold that $3 lamp of mine until he can sell it for $10." But it *is* costing him to hold that lamp, even if he just puts it on the shelf and does nothing to it—not even dust it. His money is tied up in it, earning no interest, preventing him possibly from making a more important purchase. He may have to hold it for weeks, months, even years. Antique selling is a most unpredictable business. I know right now of two beautiful pieces that are still right where I saw them more than two years ago, a Beau Brummell washstand, a little beauty and not exorbitantly priced, and a fine French brass fireplace fan screen. I don't think this particular dealer worries about them too much. She does a good business, and often a dealer likes to hold on to some things for "window dressing." But the point is they are not moving, and they do represent good cash investment.

Add to the fact that every piece a dealer sells must not only return the original investment, it must help to carry all the other expenses of the business: rent, light, heat, phone, advertising, stationery, car and hauling expenses, crating, delivery, magazines, books, breakage, insurance, accountant's fees, help in the shop or workroom, and so on. Some small businesses survive only because they are run at home and as a side line. Just recently I saw a statement by a country dealer who admitted with pride that on a year's business of $28,000 he cleared $5,000, less than 18 per cent for his whole year's work but good for net earnings. Another dealer says he can't average more than a 30 per cent to 35 per cent markup in gross earnings. A young woman who conducts a business in her home and whose husband is otherwise employed reports for the past year a net profit of 10 per cent.

I am not trying to defend the unscrupulous dealer who preys

upon ignorance, who robs the widows and orphans of their inherited treasures, offering outrageously low prices hoping he can get away with it. There are still some around, but not so many as there used to be. The sellers are getting too wary. In fact, the shoe is often on the other foot—the seller expects too much. But I do want to make it clear why you have to expect a lower price from a dealer with a profit to make than if you sell directly to a private buyer.

If you insist on selling privately, you will have to let people know in some way what you have. Word of mouth is cheap, but slow, and you have to know people interested enough to pass the word around that you are ready to sell that corner cupboard. I have bought things that way, just hearing about them. Or you can advertise. It is not worth while to do so, however, unless you have enough to sell to warrant the expense, and in that case you should know what to ask for your antiques, as it is the first question that will be put to you. You might do what two women I knew did, pooled their handful of antiques and advertised them, splitting the cost.

I am often asked, "How can I find out who the collectors are of such-and-such a thing?" You can do it in various ways. Start asking questions of dealers, of local historical societies, of the newspapers that often carry stories of local collections. You can write to various collectors' associations such as the Paperweights Collectors' Association in New York, a very active organization. There are many, many others. Some advertise in magazines such as *Hobbies* and other antique magazines. A letter to any such magazine will probably give you the information.

There are other ways of selling your antiques. You can put them into a public auction. Most auction houses will take odds and ends to work into larger sales. There are also the country auctions which occasionally fill in with outside material. I once put quite a few things into a neighbor's sale. In some parts of the country there is a weekly sale, usually on a Friday night, where things such as produce, toys, tools, furniture, handwork, etc.—and antiques are sold. You take a chance on what you may get for your pieces at such a general sale, however the dealers do watch them and you may be surprised. You pay, of course, the commission for selling, usually 20 per cent.

You can have a private sale of your own—if you have enough to dispose of. You have to advertise it, of course, and keep it going for perhaps three days, pricing everything beforehand.

Then you can put your pieces in a shop on consignment, that is, not selling them outright but giving a commission when they are sold, about 20 per cent. You and the dealer have to get together on a price that will take care of this commission. A few dealers do this to keep their shops full without putting out capital. Others won't handle it. You may find other kinds of shops that will display your things, a gift shop perhaps, a stationer's, or even the drugstore.

Other outlets for disposing of antiques are the thrift shops. They may take them on consignment or buy them outright. If these are for charity, you may not do too well here on prices. Woman's exchanges also occasionally handle antiques.

But whatever you do, don't call in the junkman! More fine antiques have escaped that way than any other.

But suppose you do not want to part with your treasures for money. What are you going to do with them? First of all, get them out of hiding, take them off that top shelf, show them off, use them if possible, or display them in style if you can't. What good does an antique do for anyone if it is hidden away in a closet, trunk, or drawer? Even valuable pieces can be displayed safely.

Just because you don't have a big collection of one thing is no reason why you should not show what you have. Set aside one place for your resurrected showpieces, a row of shelves, part of a bookcase, a room divider, window shelves or window sills, or buy an old cupboard just to show your other old pieces in. I remember when my two boys were small and I was beginning my antique scavengering. I came home one day with a huge tin coffee bin from an old store. I had got it cheap, and I was very proud of it. One boy said, "What is Mother going to do with that old thing anyway?" and the other one said with some disgust, "Aw, that's just a gadget to keep her other gadgets in."

Old frames and old clock cases make fine shadow boxes for the display of miniatures, small pieces, or one fine piece. Get the do-it-yourself man in your family to rig one up for you. Another way to show off flat pieces—old flat silver, card cases, documents, valentines, jewelry, etc., is to set them under glass in the top of a coffee table. The home workshop can make such a table from an old picture

frame with either an old or new base. Plates and platters can be
hung on the walls as you would pictures. Pitchers can be hung as a
frieze over a big window. Old fan cases are hard to find, but again
the handy man can make a protective covering for the fine old fan
from two pieces of glass set in a wooden base.

This shadow box for holding curios was once a clock case.

I am of the opinion that antiques should be used whenever possible. Of course if a thing is very valuable, rare, and falling to pieces
I would not suggest hurrying its demise, but on the whole I like to
live with my treasures, not just look at them. I like to use my daisy-
and-button goblets on my dinner table when guests come, or even
my milk-glass wineglasses when the occasion arises. Suppose someone does leave a burn on that tiptop candlestand—it was meant to
be used, wasn't it? And it isn't irreparable. Many children have
played with that old glass paperweight before I got it—and still do—
and many babies cut their teeth on the handle of that silver mug.
Antiques are things once used. Why not again?

Of course there are many old things that cannot be used in the
way they were intended to be used. Our ways of living have changed.
For instance, we don't use handleless cups or cup plates, or even
butter chips or fishbone dishes. Or hand coffee grinders or mortars
and pestles for spices. Many such things can be used for other purposes without distorting them into what I call "cute." Some of the

things turned into lamps are amusing in certain places, some are just plain awful. I can see no excuse for turning a fine old Kentucky rifle into a floor lamp, for instance. It should be hung in pride on a wall. It has enough claim to distinction. But there is no harm in using the cups and saucers from a Staffordshire toy set for after-dinner coffee, or those cut-glass penny-candy mugs for liqueurs. Any kind of odd saucer can serve out its existence as an ash tray and handleless cups as cigarette holders. Any flower arranger can tell you how welcome an antique sugarbowl, teapot, saltcellar, or pitcher can be. Two of my favorite vases were once a part of a pickle caster and a lidless cracker jar.

The best parts of old shawls, coverlets, quilts, and carpets can be used for upholstering an old chair or stool. Trivets make fine plant stands, as do those very low wooden footstools—of no other earthly use. Old washstands turn easily into cabinets for the radio or record-player, even for TV sets. A small cradle has a reason for taking up room if it is used for magazines or papers. I've seen a trundle bed plumply upholstered used in place of a modern davenport. Fine old washbasins are ideal for punchbowls, and spittoons or cuspidors turn respectable as planters. Once I found an old wooden shoe last in a trash heap. I polished it, hinged it, and used it for a door knocker on my back door.

As for furnishing with antiques, I shall go into that more fully later on. But let me say here, don't be afraid to mix your antiques with your modern pieces. A fine antique can hold up its head in almost any company. You might even feature it. Of course use restraint in pitting crude primitives against modern pieces of distinction. Keep them for special rooms. But on the whole you can scatter your Empire sofa or your Victorian armchair or your Duncan Phyfe table among your newer things and come off all right. A recent trend among the decorators is away from the stark, empty look of contemporary rooms to a cozier, lived-in atmosphere. And how are they doing it? By the use of antiques—old and interesting bric-a-brac, ornaments, and occasional pieces. So bring out your antiques. You'll be right in style.

And if you don't want to sell and aren't interested in using your old things you can always give them away and thus give pleasure to someone who can enjoy them. A friend of mine was clearing out her old home. She had some nice things. But she didn't want to sell them. "They were my mother's. I couldn't bear to think of the junkman taking them away," she told me. When I offered to buy some at a reasonable price, she still refused. "But I tell you what I'll do. You take what you want, and give me whatever you can afford to pay. I'll use it for charity in Mother's name." It was a most satisfactory arrangement for both of us.

PART II

These Are Antique

5. FURNITURE

HERE, as in most of the chapters of this book, we are going to consider only American pieces. I do not intend to dwell long on museum furniture—you can see this whenever you want to and get the story on it if you are interested. What I do want to do is to set forth the kind of things with which you are more apt to come in contact, either handed down to you or in shops or sales, and to explain their values as antiques.

Briefly, then, let us consider the course of American furniture making from the Pilgrims on to the Victorian era. When the colonists set sail for the New World they brought very few pieces in the holds of their ships, and such pieces would have been the heavy oaken Tudor or Jacobean furniture. They set their turners and joiners to work as quickly as possible making the necessary pieces for everyday living from available woods, and the results were plain and serviceable. They made three-legged stools and four-legged stools, backless benches, long, tavern-type tables, and crude cupboards, practically nothing of which remains. Back in Europe the chair was still a symbol of priority or authority, but by 1650 America was making and using its own chairs, the wainscot chair, banister-back, slat-back, armchair, all stiff and uncomfortable looking but many of them most impressive. You'll hear of the Ipswich wainscot chair, the Harvard chair of heavy "thrown" or turned oak, the Brewster chair, a simplification of the heavier Harvard chair, and the Carver chair, a heavy banister-back with rush seat. Pennsylvania had its walnut wainscot chairs with some Swedish and Dutch feeling in the lines. Virginia, too, had wainscot chairs, a straight, solid-back chair, carved or paneled. Examples of these are scattered through the museums of the country.

Furniture in these early days also included cupboards, linen presses, and the so-called "court" cupboard, which is merely a short or low cupboard. Two of the pre-1700 chests or cupboards you will hear about most often are the Hadley pieces from Hadley, Massachusetts, simple of line but elaborately if shallowly carved, and the famous Connecticut Sunflower chest. Early tables would include the stretcher table we sometimes call tavern from Pennsylvania and New England; Pilgrim "joint stools," more low tables than stools; butterfly tables with leaves and a folding wing; gate-leg tables copied so copiously; and the chair table with a tilt-back top, often called a hutch table.

From here it is a short step to the William and Mary pieces, lowboys, desks, and desks-on-frames with crisscrossed stretchers, turnip feet, and fine trumpet or cup turnings. These were made here as well as in England, and a few have escaped the museums.

But when we get to the Queen Anne period we reach a more available style that flourished in the first quarter of the eighteenth century, to my mind one of the loveliest furniture styles because of its elegance and simplicity. It is characterized by the cabriole leg (bow leg with tapering), the pad foot (sometimes a grooved variation called a Spanish foot), fan-carved motif, and delicate bailed brasses. In Queen Anne you'll find highboys, lowboys, side chairs, armchairs, and upholstered wing chairs; day beds, drop-leaf tables, and mirrors. You can buy all of these if you have enough money. Just the other day I spoke to an acquaintance who told me she owned a *pair* of matched Queen Anne tables bought not so long ago—a real triumph in antique collecting.

After Queen Anne come the stylists, Chippendale, in whose name much has been committed both good and bad, Sheraton, and Hepplewhite, all of whom worked in the middle and late Georgian periods. All of these styles overlapped. They copied, they were copied. As for Duncan Phyfe, who came later, his name is not strictly a period. He was a cabinetmaker who worked in and enriched the Directoire and Empire periods.

It was in the periods from about 1750 to 1820 that some of the finest pieces of American furniture were made. Skilled cabinetmakers in Philadelphia, Baltimore, New York, Boston, Salem, and other cities were "borrowing" and adapting the bonnet top of Queen Anne, the cabriole leg and claw and ball foot of Chippendale, the classic lines of Adam, the reeding of Sheraton, the delicacy and inlay of Hepplewhite, and the elegant features of French Directoire styles to turn out pieces strictly American, of mahogany, and American woods, mostly walnut, maple, cherry, and other fruit woods. Such pieces were being used in the cities.

Chair legs in the Hepplewhite, Sheraton, Empire, Queen Anne, and Chippendale styles.

In the country, local craftsmen fashioned simpler pieces sometimes with more primitive feeling, sometimes aping the city pieces with considerable skill, as witness the Bachman furniture from Lancaster County, Pennsylvania, which even today defies the experts to place it. This country furniture, or "cottage" furniture, or "primitives," as it is variously called, was made of pine, maple, cherry, walnut, and sometimes hickory. Often two or three woods were combined in one piece, and as often or not, perhaps for this reason, the piece was painted. It is from this group up to 1800 and later that you will get a large portion of the pieces displayed in the average antique shop or which you may still discover in your attic, cellar, or barn.

While most of the early furniture originated on the eastern coast, much of it was carried in the covered wagons to the outlying settlements, first the Middle West, then the Far West, so that good pieces are still cherished all over the country. Thus you'll find Hepplewhite in Pittsburgh, Sheraton in Cincinnati, Empire in Indianapolis, and Victorian in Davenport. On the West Coast, besides the furniture brought around the Cape, you'll find pieces of Spanish styling and in New Orleans much that is French.

Throughout this history of American furniture you will come upon whole chapters connected with a specific locality such as Shaker furniture. The Shakers migrated from England in 1770 and settled in New England, New York, Ohio, and Kentucky. They made and sold very simple, practical furniture, and because it has become scarce it is most desirable from the antique point of view. Then you have the Pennsylvania Dutch, much of it painted with the colorful peasant designs brought over with them from their home countries of Germany and Switzerland. You have Scandinavian influences in the Northwest and Holland Dutch along the Hudson River. All are American.

There are chapters not linked with stylists or localities. There is the story of the Windsor chair, named from its supposed place of origin near Windsor Castle in England. But the English variety was much heavier than the American, which began in Philadelphia and flourished in New England and New Jersey. It was perhaps the first comfortable all-wood chair in America, light and easy to move around. The broad saddle seat, the slightly tilted back (which when tall was confined in a bow, loop, or rail often with comb-back headrest), and the wide rake to the legs made it good sitting. Most of the early Windsors were painted black, dark green, red, or even white. The Philadelphia Windsor was a sturdier chair than the New England type. From New England came the bamboo-turned Windsor, the Chicken-coop railed top also called Dovecote or Birdcage. Other Windsors are known as Fanback, Butterfly, and Stepped-down, according to top-rail treatment. Windsor chairs invaded the tavern, the Congress, and the colonial home. Benjamin Franklin originated a writing-arm Windsor now owned by the University of Pennsylvania. There are, besides the original Windsor chair and settees, love seats, desk chairs, high chairs, choir chairs, and cradles, many more recent descendants of the Windsor—from the barroom or captain's chair to the common bow-back kitchen chair. If you come upon a Windsor rocking chair, however, you will probably have what was called a "converted" rocker, that is, it has rockers added, usually of the carpet-cutter type. Rocking chairs as such were not made until late in the eighteenth century whereas Windsors began their existence in America as early as 1725.

Another chapter in furniture history that will concern the seeker after antiques today is the "fancy" chair. This was the name given to a decorated side chair of all wood, wood and cane, or wood and rush, often painted or stenciled with gold. Sometimes the decoration was in the form of carving and the wood was left unpainted, as in many of the walnut chairs of the Empire period. Of them all the Hitchcock chair is perhaps the best known—a rush-bottomed chair often painted black with gold stenciling, made from about 1820 on in a small Connecticut village called Hitchcockville, later changed to Riverton. The making of these chairs has been revived today and the new ones are probably as fine as the originals. But fancy chairs went back further than Hitchcock. A lovely Adam chair of 1790 of ivory with gold decoration is called a fancy chair, as is a Pennsylvania plank-seat chair with fiddleback splat painted in the Dutch manner or stenciled. There were good ones and bad ones. Some of the Victorian side chairs were called fancy, too—and fancy they were.

Which brings us up to the era that needs some recognition—the Victorian era. Early Victorian was really a version of French antique furniture from about 1842 on. While ornate, it has some claim to beauty and grace of line. Some of the comfortable upholstered chairs, like the Prince Albert chair, the Sutherland, the Princess Adelaide, and the five-feather-shaped Prince of Wales chair, are not too unlike the French bergères. But it is the later Victorian that brings out the sneers because of its fussiness and pretentiousness. Belter Victorian furniture, while ornate, was created with care and imagination. Today a Belter piece means a good Victorian buy. It is the name Eastlake and the Gothic-revival pieces that make us shudder. Yet they are being sold, so somebody must like them.

It would be impossible to cover here a detailed history of all the phases of American furniture. There are many fine books to help you if you want to make a study of it. It is a fascinating subject. But I am going to list briefly the things you are apt to own or find on an antique safari and which you may want to identify. Chairs, you'll find, come first in availability because there were more chair-makers than other furniture artisans, and chairs were used in greater numbers. Next come the benches, sofas, and settees. Then tables, stands, sideboards, highboys and lowboys, bureaus, desks, beds, and cupboards.

Chairs

Windsors—already described.

Barroom—A form of Windsor, all wood or cane-seated with curved arms, bow back, and spindles, sometimes with a heavy rolled back or carved with a handhold. It flourished from 1870 on. Was often painted. Mostly pine.

Captain's Chair—Often confused with the barroom. Similar. Usually has a small gallery or shallow comb back over the low back rail. Another form of captain's chair has high legs, probably used in a wheelhouse. Both barroom and captain's chairs are available in the "rough" and finished. Widely reproduced.

Banister-back—An early type, high, straight back with rounded balusters or flattened ones called splats. Not easily found.

Slat-back—Often called *ladder-back* with horizontal slats across the high, straight back. Often rush-bottomed, often painted. An old type but a common one. Can still be found.

Plank-seat—General term given to all common wooden chairs with solid wood seat. Includes full spindle-back, half-spindle, arrow, curved arrow, fiddle-back, balloon-back, rabbit-ear, donkey-ear, thumb-back, and yoke-back, according to the back and post styling. Mostly pine, sometimes hickory, sometimes a combination of woods. Pine is light in weight; hickory heavy. You can get these plain or painted, single and in sets.

Wing—Upholstered with side wings, wooden legs, and sometimes with wooden arms or hand rests. The finest are Queen Anne and Chippendale. Available but costly.

Barrel—Also upholstered, but with the back curving in barrel fashion. Both wing and barrel chairs were often done in tufted leather as witness a Jefferson chair at Monticello.

Martha Washington—Sheraton armchair for ladies with upholstered seat and back and all-wood arms curved and sometimes meeting carved front posts. Widely copied.

Left, a Queen Anne wing chair. **Right,** a Martha Washington armchair.

Slipper—Low, straight-backed chair with no arms, or unobtrusive arms, upholstered back and seat. As early as Queen Anne, as late as Victorian. Sometimes called a nursing chair. Not common.

Corner—Designed to set diagonally in a corner with low back encircling two of the sides. Front leg often carved, other three plain. Seat upholstered. Originally an Adam piece. When front is rounded, called a *roundabout* chair.

Conversation—Shaped like a letter S with two chairs facing in opposite directions. A Victorian creation.

Cockfight—With narrow seat and armrest or desklike shelf on the back. To be sat in backward. Rather rare.

Sleepy Hollow—Upholstered contour lounge chair, sometimes a rocker.

Boston Rocker—This and the Salem rocker were most popular from 1830 to 1890. High-back, Windsor type; solid seat rolled at the back. Salem rocker has flat seat. Was usually painted and decorated. With or without arms. Plenty of these.

Lincoln Rocker—Upholstered parlor rocker of the 1850s. French in style, upholstered seat and back; carved arms; of rosewood, walnut, chestnut, or fruit wood. Not too hard to find.

Shaker Rocker—Slat-back with hickory splint seat or woven fabric bands or padded over rope seats. Fairly common.

Grecian Cane Rocker—Much like a Boston rocker but with cane seat and back.

Side Chairs—Of all sorts and kinds, including the "fancy" chairs described, heavy-backed Empire with upholstered seats or rush seats, Grecian chairs with curved back posts, to the armless Victorian chair of carved walnut or rosewood. Plenty to choose from.

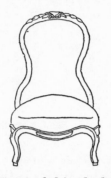

A Victorian lady's side chair.

Settees and Sofas

Sofas will be found in all the period styles: Queen Anne, Chippendale, Sheraton, Hepplewhite, Adam, Duncan Phyfe, and Empire or Directoire. Also in Victorian styles, from a carved Belter walnut or rosewood frame with three-ovaled back to a horsehair monstrosity with one tall curving end. Empire sofas often had rolled end bolsters.

Virginia Sofa—Heavy-framed sofa of mahogany of the late Empire period; carved ends and legs.

Love Seat—Upholstered settee for two in almost any of the period styles. Sometimes called a double chair.

Chair-backed Settee—Period settee with two arms and two chair backs; single upholstered seat. Not common.

Fancy Settee—Like three fancy chairs put together with single rush bottom. Not too common.

Plank Settee—Armed bench with single broad wooden seat; back spindled. Usually painted and decorated. Often a finer type, with arrow back. Plenty still around.

Left, an Empire sofa. **Right,** a painted plank settee.

Settle—Wooden bench with very high back and solid winged sides for the fireside to keep off drafts. Early and primitive.

Bench Table—Wooden bench with a pegged-on top that makes a back and drops for a table top. Available.

Windsor Settee—Low-backed wooden spindled settee with eight legs and perhaps bamboo-turned spindles. Straight or curved arms or bow back. Love seat rare. Painted or of natural wood. Pine as a rule. Ten-leg scarce. Possible to find but not common.

Window Bench—Backless bench or stool, often upholstered, sometimes with ends, in various period styles. Also used for fireside. Can be found.

Church Bench—Continually showing up as old churches are modernized. Meetinghouse benches very stiff and quaint. Often painted.

Stools

There were upholstered stools in all periods. Original coverings were of petit point, tapestry, brocade, or crewel or flame-stitch embroidery. They were round, oblong, square, and often came in pairs. The Empire footrest with rolled ends is most familiar. Woods were walnut, mahogany, or cherry. Frames were sometimes equipped with slip cushions. Good frames, if found, can be used for new needlework.

Ottoman—Round, square, or oblong all-upholstered stool. Victorian. Reupholstered, can be made quite interesting.

Painted Stools—These are usually of Pennsylvania Dutch origin. They have low wooden ends rather than feet. Not too common.

Crickets—A church kneeling stool or any small legged stool.

Footrests—Very low, designed to keep the feet off the floor away from drafts. Pine and primitive. Available.

Tables and Stands

Drop-leaf—Found in all periods from Queen Anne to the common kitchen table with rounded leaves. Most desirable in mahogany or cherry or maple. Not too often found in pine. Many in walnut. Depth of leaf adds to value; also turning of the legs. Found oftener with six legs, two swinging out to support leaves when raised. Four-legged table has swinging brace to support leaves, or in small, fine tables two alternate legs swing out. If you plan to buy one for a dining table, be sure to calculate where the legs fall for comfortable sitting. Plenty to choose from.

Pembroke—Small drop-leaf, originally a breakfast table. In fine woods and period styles. Four legs. Leaves straight and shallow, oval or serpentine. Usually braced. Not common but available.

Tea Table—Like the Pembroke. In earlier period leaves were supported by two of the four legs. Other tea tables are porringer-topped with rounded extensions on the corners to support silver or pewter porringers. Also a tray-top table, small and low. Fairly rare.

Dining Table—Early types were enlarged by setting one or more tables between the two end tables which were often semicircular console type. Later models, like Duncan Phyfe, were extension tables. All fine; mostly mahogany. Available but costly.

Card Table—Made in all periods. Usually found with fold-over leaf and additional leg or brace. When closed, makes a fine console or wall table. Available especially in later styles.

Corner Table—A triangular table with a triangular leaf that lifts to make a square top. In Queen Anne and other styles. Rare.

Sofa Table—Very much like the reproductions seen today. Long with small drop leaves on ends. To set behind sofa. All periods.

Serving Table—Narrow table, often marble-topped, used before sideboards and also with sideboards. All periods. Not common.

Gate-leg—Familiar because widely reproduced in modern furniture. Drop leaves and swing-out two-legged section with stretchers for bracing. Some very early tables were gate-legs. Costly if you find them.

Butterfly—Old type and rare though also copied. Stretcher base with splayed legs and butterfly wings to support the drop leaves. Usually small. Primitive.

Tavern—A sturdy table, very primitive, in oak or pine with stretchers running close to the floor around the outside of the legs to serve as footrests. Also called a *stretcher table*. Some were made of walnut. A *high-low stretcher table* has side stretchers higher than the end ones. All usually have drawers. A *trestle* table has one lengthwise member supporting end trestles.

Moravian Table—Simple four-legged stand with two drawers, large pegged top with sleigh runners like the top of a bench table. Pine and primitive. Many such tables have breadboard ends and occasionally extension end pieces to be slipped on in wooden grooves for lengthening the table. A farm piece. Can be found.

Hutch Table—Name often given to a tilt-top chair table but more rightly the table that is a dough box on legs.

Sawbuck Table—Familiar picnic-type table in tavern size—another farm table. Usually of pine, occasionally of walnut. Might have a scalloped apron. Not too common.

Harvest Table—Long, narrow table with shallow drop leaves. Usually pine. Designed to take up little room between use. Quite a few.

Lazy Susan—Round table with revolving section in center for easy serving. Much copied. Usually pine. Available.

Tilt-top—Graceful table with hinged top that tilts to vertical position. All periods and in fine woods, mostly mahogany. Usually round but occasionally square. *Tilt-and-turn* not only tilts but top can be turned to suit the position of the legs. *Dish-top* has a slightly raised edge to keep liquids from spilling off table. *Piecrust* is a crinkled raised edge. Available.

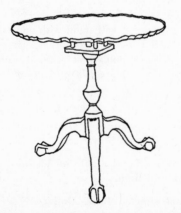

A Chippendale tilt-and-turn bird-cage table.

Drum Table—Has a round top, deep drawers in apron on a four-legged pedestal. Used as a small side table or sewing table. Period styles. Not common.

Sewing Table—Many varieties and of all periods. What we call the Martha Washington table so often reproduced is a Sheraton style with two end wells as well as drawers. Others have two or three drawers on a pedestal base. Some have a tambour closing instead of drawers or under the drawers. *Bandbox* table has deep pleated or shirred material section under the drawered top stretched on a bandbox-shaped frame.

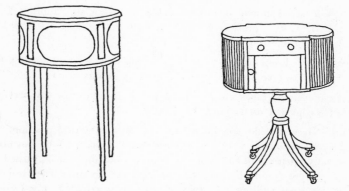

Left, a Duncan Phyfe drum table. *Right*, a tambour sewing table.

Bedside Table or *Nightstand*—Small stand with one or two drawers, sometimes with none. All periods. Woods range from mahogany, cherry, curly maple, to pine and poplar. Very fine or quite primitive. A few may have shelves with scalloped edges. Plenty of these to choose from.

Spool Table—Of the same period as the spool bed, a popular style of the the 1880s and nineties. These are the Victorian tea tables or side tables with oblong or oval top, and legs and stretchers turned to resemble a string of spools. Often with drawers. Common.

Center Table—The round family table of Victorian homes with heavy pedestal base. All you want.

Eastlake Table—Marble-topped, fussy, Gothic-revival style of Victorian table. Awful but much in demand. Probably walnut.

Candlestand—Except for early primitive holders of iron or wood this usually means a small round-topped pedestal table just big enough to hold a candle and perhaps a Bible.

Dough-box Table—Coffin-shaped box with lid and legs. Primitive. Pine. Available.

Washstand—In many early and late styles and all periods to hold pitcher and basin. Best are the corner stands of fine woods like mahogany and satinwood with holes for basin, mugs, etc. Also primitive pieces in the same style painted to match cottage bedroom sets. Victorian washstands usually matched the bedroom set and can be pretty awful or redeemable for other uses. Marble-topped ones are desirable for serving tables or bars. Popular and still available are the lift-top commodes with chamber compartment below, and a drawer. Pine, as a rule, and found in New York and New England. Also popular is the small stand with towel bars at the sides.

Left, a Chippendale fire screen. *Right,* a candlestand.

Dressing Table—Small stand with drawers, mirror either on separate frame or incorporated with it. Often is the lift-top type with mirror inside the top. *Beau Brummell* is the name given to a man's dressing table with many compartments and a washbasin in a drawer. Such pieces are usually fine, especially the Sheraton pieces. Similar is the *Captain's Dresser Chest*. A few around.

Cobbler's Bench—Low workbench and seat with storage bins and drawers. Pine. Crude. Not made as furniture but used nowadays as a coffee table. You can get them if you want them.

Fire Screens—An adjustable shield on a footed base for shielding the face from the open fire. Most available are Chippendale with tapestry or petit-point scene picture.

Dumb Waiter or *Muffin Stand*—Three-tiered stand for serving refreshments or tea. This has also been called a Lazy Susan. All periods. In mahogany, cherry, maple, and pine. Also in the Victorian era in iron. Available.

Whatnot—Better name is *étagère*. Tiered set of shelves for displaying bric-a-brac. Empire or Victorian. Sometimes spool-turned.

Canterbury—Actually a music holder. Now reproduced for holding magazines or papers in a vertical position. Some very fine in period styles.

Sideboards

Sideboards did not exist before the Hepplewhite period. Before that a side table flanked by a pair of urn-topped cupboards was used. The best are Hepplewhite and Sheraton. Other periods represented are Directoire, Empire, and Victorian. Typical Victorian sideboard has a marble top, many tiers of shelves, and much carving. Probably walnut. You can always buy a fine sideboard if you want to pay the price.

Left, a Sheraton sideboard. *Right,* a plain hunt table.

Hunt Table—A southern type of sideboard often quite plain and quite high because food was served from it buffet style to standing guests on hunt days. Woods were cherry, walnut, mahogany, pine, and tulip-wood.

Highboys, Lowboys, Bureaus, and Chests

Highboy—A tall drawered chest standing quite high on a table-type base; six legs in William and Mary pieces, four on all others. All periods up to Directoire. Fine pieces in fine woods. A Philadelphia highboy is the ultimate. Getting rarer and rarer.

Left, a Queen Anne highboy. *Right,* a William and Mary lowboy.

Lowboy—A low chest resembling the lower half of a highboy.

Chest-on-chest—also called a *Double Chest.* Tall drawered piece with the base not a table type but another larger drawered chest; division clearly recognizable. All periods. Fine woods. A bit easier to find than a highboy.

Bureaus—Chests of drawers, flat top, bureau height, all periods, including bow front, break front, serpentine, bombé, block front, carved, columned, inlaid, of infinite variety up to the Victorian marble-topped piece with attached mirror. Also primitive style in simple pine cottage chest of drawers, sometimes painted.

Linen Press—Tall wardrobe type with doors; shelves inside. Early and rare.

Kas—Dutch name for a very large press or cupboard made in the Hudson Valley area and in Pennsylvania. Used as a clothes press with two doors and large drawers underneath. Often painted in fruit and swag patterns. Rare but available.

Blanket Chest—A low, lift-top chest with or without drawers often called a *Dower Chest* or *Marriage Chest*. In the Pennsylvania Dutch country painted with peasant designs. Often has a money till hidden inside. Another form of blanket chest looks like a four-drawer chest but two upper drawers are fake. Called a *Mule Chest.*

Left, a painted Pennsylvania Dutch chest. **Right,** a painted Victorian cottage bureau and mirror.

Court Cupboard—Name given to another form of press with door or doors above and drawers below. Early and rare. Name is also used for any small cupboard or wardrobe with two doors—court meaning short or low.

Desks

Desk Box—Slope-front box to be set on top of a table or chest—early ones very rare. However, this type of desk was revived in the nineteenth century and was often called a *lap desk*, sometimes a *field desk*. Could be quite fine, of mahogany, walnut, or bird's-eye maple. Can be found.

Desk-on-frame—Very early, really a desk box set on its own frame or table. William and Mary or Queen Anne periods. Perhaps never made in America. Very rare.

Slope-fall Desk—Model for many desks from Queen Anne up to the present day. Also called a *slant-top desk*. Front falls down to make writing shelf. All woods, primitive pieces as well as fine period pieces. Erroneously called Governor Winthrop desk—no such thing.

Left, a break-front secretary. *Center*, a block-front secretary. *Right*, a slant-top desk.

Table Desk—The other most popular type of desk. A flat-topped piece made in all periods. Kneehole is a variation on the style with space for the knees between two tiers of drawers. This type as well as the slope-fall desk had bow fronts with single convex curve, serpentine with double curve, block front with drawer surface alternately recessed and projected, break front where front is not a continuous line, and bombé, a pear-shaped bulbous shape with sides swelling to wider proportions at base.

Secretary—Any of the above types with cupboard added. Glass doors or wooden doors or even mirrored doors. All periods right up to the Victorian. Available.

Tambour Desk—A desk where inside pigeonholes, etc., are hidden by a sliding tambour screen. Wide front shelf used for writing space often hinged in center to be folded back. Mostly Sheraton and Hepplewhite. Best features of these periods. Not common.

Butler's Desk—A name often given to a bureau desk where the top drawer front drops down for a writing shelf. Probably an Empire or Victorian piece. Available.

Countinghouse Desk—Large flat-top desk with slanted writing shelf in center; pigeonholes across the back. Usually high, requiring a stool. Also called a *storekeeper's desk.*

School Desk—Simple desk on legs. Slant top lifts up rather than falls down. Usually has a drawer and is usually pine. Not a desk for easy writing, though it can be adapted. Plenty of these.

A school desk.

Ladies' Desk—Victorian type of slant top, small and dainty. Or it might be what is called a *student's desk* with a straight fall front like a small secretary.

Beds

Four-poster—A bed with either tall or low posts made in all periods up to late Empire. Earlier ones are very fine. Made in all woods including pine and maple. To be had, but you might have to wait for the one you want.

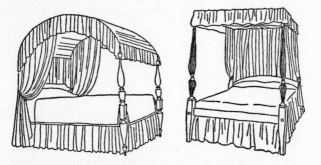

Left, a field bed. Right, a canopied four-poster.

Tester Bed—A tall four-poster with frame at top to hold a valance.

Field Bed—A tall four-poster of light proportions equipped with an arched frame on which material is shirred for canopy.

Half-canopy—Bed with an awninglike top extending only from the two headposts. Not common.

Folding Bed—A bed that lifts up and stands straight against a wall behind curtains or cupboard. Very early ones rare. Victorian folding beds were apt to be hidden in anything.

Trundle Bed—A very low bed to be slipped under a high bed. Used as an extra bed or for children. You can find them occasionally.

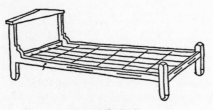

A trundle bed.

Day Bed—A narrow bed with one slanted chair-back end for lounging. All periods. Some very fine with rush or cane bottoms or cushioned. Possible to find.

Sleigh Bed—Of the Empire period. With heavy rolled head and footboards, both rolling out. Occasionally you'll find one with the foot rolling in. Available.

Spool Bed—Cottage type with spool turnings or button turnings. Sometimes with solid or scrolled headboard. Called a *Jenny Lind* bed. Pine, maple, or poplar. Were often painted.

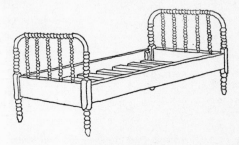

A Jenny Lind bed.

Rope Bed—Most early beds before the time of wire bedsprings were rope beds equipped with pegs on the top, bottom, and sides around which rope could be caught to make a crisscrossed webbing for the mattress to rest upon. Sometimes a piece of stout canvas or sacking was roped on for the same purpose, to give resiliency.

Iron and Brass Beds—They are coming back into favor. Victorian and often not too much of an eyesore. The lacy scrolled kind fit in with new metal *décor*.

Victorian Bed—This was the very ornate, high headboard bed of walnut. Many have been cut up to make other furniture.

Cupboards

Corner Cupboard—A cupboard made with three sides, to fit into a corner. Big storage space and took up little room. Range from very fine mahogany or walnut period pieces to simple one-door, solid-wood pine kitchen cupboard. Many with two doors above and cupboard space below. With and without drawers. Solid wood or glass-paned doors; panes at top plain or arched. Fine type is the arched shell and dome interior with pilaster sides. Another has the famous thirteen-light door (from the thirteen original states). Many old cupboards have butterfly shelves and spoon notches. Also found painted in some parts of the country. All periods. All woods. Famous painted piece is a Mahantango Valley cupboard painted in the Pennsylvania Dutch fashion.

Wall Cupboard or *Welsh Cupboard*—A type of kitchen cupboard that sets straight against the wall. Has no doors and often is embellished with a scalloped border. Shelves above; drawers and cupboard space below. Many reproductions.

Hanging Cupboard—Wall type or corner type. No base. Some very early pieces in pine or walnut. Sometimes painted and decorated. Usually with solid wood door. May have lower open shelf or swing-out wooden drawers.

Pie Cupboard or *Pie Safe*—A country piece usually of pine. Narrow cupboard with many shelves. Door may be of pierced tin. *Milk cupboard* similar. Occasionally hanging type.

Jelly Cupboard—Much like the pie cupboard, only larger. Another primitive piece. Pine or poplar. Sometimes has two drawers above the cupboard space. Kitchen piece.

Dry Sink—A country piece of pine, maple, or birch, cupboard below but open zinc-lined trough above for washing dishes. May have small drawers at top.

A dry sink.

Water Bench—Shallow stand with or without drawers and cupboard space to hold pails of water or milk. Available.

Cradles

Rockaby Cradle—Earliest of the rocking type was a box set on rockers, often with a hood. Primitive pine cradle with slats in the bottom had pegs for roping in the baby. Not hard to find.

Bassinet—A stationary cradle in a frame with much drapery; also a handled wicker basket like a clothes basket but with one end higher than the other.

Swinging Cradle—In Sheraton's manual this was called the "swinging crib bed." It was hung on posts and goes back to Queen Anne period. Sheraton invented a spring to be wound up that would keep the cradle swinging for more than an hour. Some Victorian swinging cradles were "stoppered" to keep them from tipping over. All you want.

Mammy Chair—A rocking chair bench with one end for the "sitter" and the other railed to make a cradle. Another version is a rocking chair with an extension that pulls out for a cradle. Not too common.

Mirrors

Wall Mirror—This follows all the fine furniture styles. In early mirrors glass was often in two parts because it was imported here and taxed in England, and small pieces were cheaper. Often combined with painted picture-glass panel. Some of the finest carvings and moldings

Left, a Chippendale fretwork mirror. **Right,** a convex or bull's-eye mirror.

and gilt on the best ones. Chippendale made an oval mirror but most mirrors were long and narrow. The Constitution mirror of mahogany with scrolled pediment and gilded eagle, urn, or vase at the top is often copied. Primitive pine mirrors with crude pictures aped the finer ones. Plenty to choose from if you don't want them too rare or early.

Overmantel Mirror—Low and wide, sometimes in three sections. Frame usually gold. Can be found.

Courting Mirror—A small mirror in mirrored frame. Brought over from China to New England and thus has Chinese feeling in the painted glass flowers and unusual woods. Very fine. Not too easy to find.

Convex Mirror or *Bull's-eye Mirror*—Elaborate gold-framed mirror with convex glass that reflects a diminished scene like wide-vision lens. Sometimes called a *Butler's Mirror* because with it the butler behind his screen could keep an eye on the whole dining room. Much reproduced.

Girandole—A convex mirror with candle sconces. Possible to find.

Shaving Mirror—A small tilting mirror on its own stand with or without a drawer to be used on top of a chest or bureau. You can find them.

A shaving mirror of the 1800s.

6. GLASS

WHEN I think of the books and books that have been written on the various phases of American glass I hesitate to try to give such a brief summary of it. However, this chapter is intended only as a lead into the subject, a directive to what you may want to know and to help you find out the rest of the story for yourselves. Of all the topics covered by the words "American antique," glass would seem to offer the most material to pull upon with the possible exception of furniture. For in telling the story of American glass we have far less confusion with imports of foreign origin though naturally some foreign glass, Irish Waterford, English pieces as well as Swedish and German, did come into the colonies. Most of it, however, is fairly easy to recognize. And, strangely enough, there is, in spite of its fragility, much fine American glass to illustrate the history of its progress, although the supply is being rapidly exhausted and many reproductions are oozing into the market to replace it.

America began to make its own glass almost immediately. Proof exists of glass factories in the Jamestown, Salem, New Amsterdam, and Philadelphia settlements, but none of this early glass remains to tell the story of just what it was, probably only bottles and window glass. And so we begin with the names of Wistar, Stiegel, and

Amelung, all of whom flourished before 1800. In the early days of the colonies glass was imported from England, Ireland, and France, and was very much of a luxury. Very little was used by the people as a whole. Tableware was made of pewter, wood, or pottery. In fact, England forbade the making of glass in this country.

In 1739 Caspar Wistar, a brass button maker of Philadelphia, defied the parent country and with some friends established a glass factory in Salem County, southern New Jersey, in a settlement he called Wistarberg. The plant set out originally to make the much-needed window glass and bottles. Wistar imported foreign workers, mostly German, for workmen. It is interesting to note that most early glassworkers were brought over from countries where glassmaking was a highly developed art—Germany, Italy, the Lowlands, and the British Isles—which accounts for the close resemblance our early products had to European glass.

South Jersey glass, as the output of Wistar and Stanger who followed quickly on his heels is known, was blown glass, as was all the earliest glass, what is known as free-blown, or blown into a part-size or dip mold at some point in the blowing, merely to shape the piece or to suggest a pattern which was almost lost in the subsequent blowing. This is quite different from the blown-three-mold method which followed later. Here the glass was blown into a three-part mold the size of the finished piece and the pattern was definitely impressed. Patterns in blown-three-mold will show concavely on the inside of the piece. A third method produced what was called pressed glass, and was accomplished by pressing the molten glass in a mold manipulated by a handle. Classification of glass according to method of decoration brings out such things as overlay, applied, etched, cut, stippled, and so on.

A South Jersey lily-pad mug.

This first South Jersey glass was a sturdy ware made from bottle glass, free-blown, freely shaped and ornamented. It was graceful in shape and decoration. Colors ran from clear through all the greens, from pale aquamarine to deep olive green, amber, blue (artificially added), but no red or amethyst. The most outstanding decoration was the applied swirl called a lily pad.

Now this glass did not stay put in one factory or even in one region. As in so many other glass factories, workmen left, made new affiliations, and took their methods and patterns with them, putting out products almost identical with the original ones, sometimes better. And so today the experts will not commit themselves to identifying positively a piece as Wistar or even South Jersey. What they say is that it is South Jersey-type. They do the same with Stiegel, who followed forty years later, and with Nicholas Lutz, who came a whole century later.

The story of Baron Stiegel is one of pure romance. Even the title was merely a courtesy. No more colorful figure has emerged from the history of the American glass industry. He came to America from Rotterdam in 1750, a young man of twenty-one. In two years he had married the daughter of a prosperous ironmaster of Pennsylvania and was made a partner. In five years he had his own place, Elizabeth Furnace, and began experimenting with glass as well as making iron. He brought over a colony of German and English workmen, laid out a whole town for them called Mannheim, and built himself a mansion there. His living was on a comic-opera scale. But his glory did not last long. His business crashed in 1774. He was imprisoned for bankruptcy and spent the later years of his life as a foreman in one of his own plants and in teaching the music he had always loved. He lies in an unmarked grave.

But from this man's dizzy endeavors has come some of the finest of American glass. Again it did not stay in one factory. His workmen moved westward to Pittsburgh and Ohio. Of course it is evident that Stiegel "borrowed" from the glass of the Old World as he remembered it and through the techniques of his workmen, but nevertheless it is an American product conditioned by its times. Stiegel was of both the flint and the soda-lime variety, the best being of light weight with a delicacy of texture and a thin, brilliant surface hard to find in early glass. Colors were deep and uniform, a deep rich blue being most characteristic, although Stiegel was made in green, wine, and amethyst as well as in clear glass. It was engraved, enameled in peasant designs, sometimes flecked with opaque white, and occasionally bicolored.

Stiegel pieces included (as listed in old bills and statements) gallon jugs for wine, cider, and vinegar; quart, half-pint, pint, gill, and half-gill glasses; flip glasses for the spiced ale of the period; saltcellars, cream pitchers, sugarbowls with finial-tipped lids; sylla-bub and jelly glasses; wineglasses with "cotton" spiral or air-twist stems; decanters; inkpots; flowerpots; lemonade jars; mustard pots; candlesticks and gemels. These were all sold cheaper than the English imports and were welcomed by the colonists. To own a piece of this genuine Stiegel is a triumph but not an impossibility.

Stiegel glass: a saltcellar in clear glass, an engraved wineglass, an enameled bottle.

Not two miles from where I live there is an original Stiegel salt-cellar which the owner will not sell for any price, and another neigh-bor within calling distance has a blue Stiegel bowl which has come down in the family from Mannheim days. However, most of the true Stiegel, also the Stiegel-type, is in museums or the hands of collectors, although occasionally a good piece pops up on the market.

The third great name in American glass is that of John Frederick Amelung whose New Bremen glassworks at Frederick, Maryland, operated from 1785 to 1794. Not much of the finest Amelung lives to tell the tale, and what does is mostly museum property and highly prized. The recent discovery of another Amelung "presentation" lidded goblet made headlines. Amelung glass pieces show beautiful workmanship reminiscent of Irish glass of the period, deeply engraved with copper wheels by skilled artisans. The soda-lime composition of the glass gives it a grayish, greenish tint. Some Amelung pieces were dated and signed and thus act as guides to the unsigned pieces.

Now during these seventy-five years other glassworks were springing up all over the colonies. By 1800 the Stiegel tradition had been carried as far as Ohio in which state Zanesville became a center and gave its name to the glass made there. Glass was being made in Philadelphia, Baltimore, Pittsburgh, Boston, and Sandwich, not to

A blown-three-mold sugar bowl.

mention smaller communities in Ohio, New York, Connecticut, New Hampshire, and Vermont. From 1810 to 1817 there were at least thirty-eight glass factories flourishing in the country, all making varying qualities of blown glass. It was not until 1820 that blown-three-mold glass began to be made. It was a distinctive American product probably designed to imitate the fine wheel-cut designs imported from England and Ireland. Names connected with this type of glass are Coventry (Connecticut), Keene (New Hampshire), and Mount Vernon (New York). Today there are admittedly 145 patterns of this glass although there may be still more undiscovered. Commoner patterns show reeding, quilting, and sunburst. All kinds of tableware were made: mugs, flips, tumblers, pitchers, sugarbowls, plates, bowls, saltcellars, and celery vases. Of particular note are the handsome decanters, but there were also toilet bottles, caster bottles, inkwells, hats, candlesticks, and peg lamps.

Pressed glass came into manufacture as early as 1829, offering a quicker, cheaper way to make glass on a commercial scale. A glassmaker named Deming Jarvis with the New England Glass Company took out a patent for a handled press and gave the new idea a push toward big production when he went over to the Boston and Sandwich Glass Company. Soon pressed glass raged through the country like a forest fire with at least fifteen factories making it by 1837. The first pressed glass was lacy glass, so called because of its fine lacelike patterns and stippled background. Lacy glass has become almost synonymous with cup plates—those handy little table adjuncts for holding the handleless tea or coffee cup while the beverage was drunk out of the saucer. It was used for many other pieces too—large plates, platters, pitchers, sugarbowls, covered dishes, compotes, salt-cellars, and celery dishes. However, it is the cup plates that have become the pets of the collectors. More than 1,000 patterns are known to have been made. This first pressed glass was lead glass of fine quality which had a brilliance only because of the sharp and faceted patterning. Lacy Sandwich as well as lacy glass from other factories is still available, but because it has been widely reproduced it requires care in selection. Also plenty of cold cash.

Lacy Sandwich cup plates.

When we progress to the pattern glass, as we call it today, we are plunging into a wilderness of patterns which may not even yet be wholly discovered. Glass experts class the patterns with varying degrees of accuracy, according to dates. The earliest comprise the classic and to my mind the most beautiful patterns such as Ashburton, Argus, Excelsior, Colonial, Flute, Loop, Pillar, Cable, Huber, Thumbprint, Diamond Thumbprint, Waffle Thumbprint, Diamond Point, Diamond Block, and Washington. There may be some confusion of names between the original ones and the names used today. I don't doubt but that this holds true all along the line of identifying pattern glass, particularly when new unnamed patterns turn up.

Some of the most popular patterns belong in the groups made from 1840 to 1860, more elaborate designs such as Comet, Horn of Plenty, Fleur de Lis, New England Pineapple, as well as the ribbed patterns, Bellflower, Ivy, Grape, Acorn, Ribbed Palm, and Inverted Fern. In the 1860s came the well-known Lincoln Drape, Cable, Roman Key, Frosted Tulip, etc. By 1870 patterns grew more elaborate yet, and we find Westward Ho!, Lion, Three Faces, Thousand Eye, Hobnail, Daisy and Button, Shell and Tassel, and many others not to mention their variations. Ruth Webb Lee, the high priestess of pattern glass, has listed more than 300 patterns of pressed tableware with many more of which only a piece or two have been found.

Pressed glass: a Lion compote, a "Give Us This Day" bread tray, a Lincoln Drape compote, a Peacock Feather lamp.

Pressed glass was made not only in the clear glass but in many colors and variations of colors: canary, vaseline and amber, a pale yellowish green as well as a deeper jade green, turquoise, cobalt, and electric blue, amethyst to purple, as well as opaque colors, white (milk glass), opalescent, "camphor," "custard," "clam broth," blue, green, marbled (slag), in caramel and purple, and many others. But not all patterns were made in all colors. The combination of color and pattern has a lot to do with the value of any piece, some pieces

being much rarer than others. On the whole, the colored pieces are
considerably higher than the clear.

A notched-edge slag platter.

A word about milk glass—or more correctly opaque white. This
has been a favorite with collectors for many years, but it has been
reproduced to such a point that it is a risk to buy it unless you know
its origin, although an expert can usually spot the difference. Here
are the animal covered dishes, the hens, swans, horses, kittens, owls,
the classic fluted bowls, the S-border, 1,000-eye border or Gothic
plates, many showing the remnants of old paint and gilt when they
were threaded with ribbon to be hung on the wall. Here are some
of the most beautiful of the old kerosene lamp bases and dolphin
candlesticks. Here, too, are the later Victorian pieces, the dresser
sets, clocks, match safes, holy-water fonts, souvenir hatchets, etc.,
much of which is fine, some not so fine, but all in great demand.

Milk glass lamp base, plate, and pitcher.

What has made this pattern glass produced in such profusion so valuable? It is not hard to explain the high prices for the earlier varieties of fine quality because with age the supply is giving out. But many of us still living and not so old can remember using the later patterns, eating our rice pudding from a vaseline footed saucedish or drinking our milk from a Rose-in-Snow goblet, while we listened to the story of how these pieces were given away with baking powder or tea or raffled off at the band hall after a Saturday-night concert. Why is this once commonplace glass so sought after now? Well, in the first place, it is—or was—easily obtainable. With diligent search one can still fill out a whole table service in one pattern, even though the earlier and more popular ones are scarce. Much of it has charm. It is nostalgic, it goes with other American pieces better than new glass. Add to this that for a long time, since the thirties at least, it has been a fad, an excuse to go "looking" and poking into the antique shops. Many women have been introduced to antiques in general through the exciting pursuit of pressed glass. It is the kind of thing that is most apt to come out of the china closets and homes built before 1900. It is not to be scorned by any means, but it does require good taste and a sense of selection to pick the best.

A late group of American glass is the art glass, the "fancy" glass of the 1880s, nineties, and early 1900s. This includes many memorable pieces also, the ornaments that stood on the parlor mantelpiece or whatnot. It has its place in the story of American glass because it produced some very fine examples of glassmaking. It began with the sale of a Chinese vase of the Tang period at the Morgan sale of 1886, which was copied by the Mount Washington Glassworks of New Hampshire and in Wheeling, West Virginia. The very creditable copy was called Peach Blow, a lovely ware, sometimes satiny, sometimes glossy, shading from rose-red to pale yellow and usually cased over a white lining.

Close to this comes Amberina, another shaded glass, also Burmese, running from salmon pink to lemon yellow. Satin glass has a soft mat finish, is often quilted, sometimes shaded, of various colors, and usually cased. Mother-of-pearl is a variation of this. Other types of art glass include Spangled Glass flecked with color in spatter effect, Agata, a mottled glass, Vasa Murrhina with imbedded variegated colors, and the famous Nicholas Lutz glass with its beautiful threads, stripes, and applied decorations. This artist served an apprenticeship in France and worked at the Sandwich factory. His delicate creations come close to fine Venetian glass. Unless you find them signed it is safer to call such pieces Lutz-type.

Art glass: a Peach Blow vase, a Tiffany vase, a Lutz-type cruet, a Mary Gregory bottle.

In this same category is the Mary Gregory glass, so named for the artist whose white applied figures decorate the dark glass of green, blue, or cranberry. Her figures were usually of children at play and are most pleasing. Other names on the art glass list are Cameo, Pomona, Kewblas, Aurene, and Tortoise Shell.

To many the name of Tiffany means jewels. Yet an early Tiffany, son of the original jeweler in New York, established a factory on Long Island in 1890 for the manufacture of a ware called Favrile. His glass showed the influence of early study of stained glass in France, for it had a brilliant iridescence, much gold, and rich colorings. Many Tiffany pieces are marked. Quezal was an imitation of Tiffany and was also marked.

Bottles

Through the entire history of glass in America bottles were being made. The bottle collector has a long range to roam if he does not narrow down his search. Many early bottles were designed for wine and spirits in various sizes. (See Stiegel output.) Earlier bottles were

inclined to be squattier than later ones, or else very tall and thin.
Bottles have taken on such names as Hogarth, Ludlow, chestnut,
case, and saddle, according to shape and use. There were early blown
bottles for medicine, for commodities like oil, snuff, perfume, smelling salts, blacking, and the same in the blown-mold type. Bitters
bottles designed for various "patent medicines" with high alcoholic
content in the 1860s and 1870s are a class unto themselves.

Flasks

These are the whisky bottles, flat-sided probably to slip easily
into a greatcoat pocket and with shorter necks for tippling. You
will meet here the Pitkin flask, supposedly the first of this type to
be manufactured at the Pitkin Glassworks in East Manchester, New
Hampshire, early in the nineteenth century but made at other

Flasks.

places, too. Here are the portrait flasks with emphasis on the Washington flasks of many variations. The faces of Adams, Jackson,
Harrison, and Taylor appeared on flasks as did those of Benjamin
Franklin, Lafayette, Clay, Dewitt Clinton, Jenny Lind, Major Ring-
gold, and Kossuth. All these flasks come in many variations, com-
binations, shapes, and sizes. Other flask decoration went in for
eagles, the flag, Columbia, Masonic emblems, slogans, railroads, and
Pikes Peak. Flasks were shaped like bellows and violins, were round
or calabash-shaped, showed cornucopia or sunburst impressions—a
fascinating array in colors from pale aqua to deep olive green. You
can still buy old flasks, but you can also buy out-and-out fakes. Study
them and be careful.

Character Bottles

Here is an interesting side line of bottle collecting. It embraces all those bottles designed for various purposes but fashioned in the shape of objects or human figures or animals. Thus you have fish

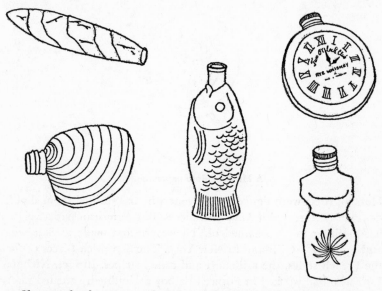

Character bottles: cigar, corked clam shell, fish, "naughty lady," watch.

bottles, cigars, watches, pretzels, pigs, elephants, potatoes, Santa Claus, Carry Nation, crying baby, naughty lady, treetrunks, clam shells, slippers, pistols, and hands, to name a few. They are amusing —but that is all. The Booz bottle and the Tippecanoe log cabin bottle are "character" bottles after a fashion, but they mean more historically.

Other Collectible Bottles

Of great interest are many other bottles both early and late, the small medicine phials carried by doctors in their cases, nursing bottles, preserve jars and pickle bottles, glass store jars of all kinds, apothecary bottles, barber bottles, soda-pop bottles, and so on.

Paperweights

It is easy to go quite haywire over paperweights—if you have the money to indulge yourself. These "frozen jewels" number some of the most beautiful of glass creations. The best and earliest were made in France, at Baccarat, St. Louis, and Clichy from 1840 on.

A Millville Rose paperweight.

Many of these were signed and anyone who has studied them should not confuse them with American pieces. But American paperweights had nothing to be ashamed of. They were first made at Sandwich and by John J. Gilliland in New York. The Sandwich pieces copied the French styles, the millefiori and candy stripes. In fact, Nicholas Lutz who had worked in France as a boy undoubtedly created many of them. Other early pieces showed flowers and fruit frozen in the fine flint glass. Green glass turtle weights were made from 1865 to 1870. At Millville, New Jersey, many fine paperweights were turned out, among them the famous Millville Rose made by the perfectionist Ralph Barber; his yellow rose on a footed base is a choice piece. There were weights with scenes, animals, snakes, seals, portraits, and historical or allegorical medallions in their composition, and some even with mottoes. Paperweights made cheap souvenir pieces of which the little snowstorm piece is an example. You might have to pay more than $2,000 for a St. Louis faceted weight but you can find plenty of interesting ones for $5. Of the same style of glass wizardry are vases, candlesticks, inkstands, wig stands, and doorknobs. Old weights may show a smoothed-off pontil mark or a cut star on the base. Frosted bases are usually new.

This and That

Other glass objects to keep in mind when reviewing the story of American glass are drawer knobs, curtain tiebacks, and mirror knobs, many of them of opalescent Sandwich and made for pewter screws. Still other articles you are apt to come upon are:

Smoke Bells—Graceful lily-shaped glass bells to be hung over a lamp to avoid smoking the ceiling. Clear colors and opaque.

Bride's Baskets—Ruffle-edged baskets of colored glass often set in a silver frame. Favorite wedding present from 1880 to 1900. Reproduced.

Mercury Glass—Silver glass made by filling two layers of clear glass with a silver solution. Mantel ornaments, vases, doorknobs, etc.

End-of-day—Pieces supposedly made at the end of a workman's day for his own amusement. Includes novelties like hats, slippers, shoes, etc., for matches or toothpicks. Term is also given to a mottled glass supposedly made from the remnants of colors left at the end of a work day. Both interpretations of the term are disputed.

Coin Glass—Produced in 1892 and incorporated in the patterns real United States coins all dated 1892 except a half dime. The United States Treasury stopped production of it after only five months. Rare and desirable.

Bristol Glass—Original Bristol glass was made in England but a similar glass was produced here. A frosted glass with painted and applied decorations, often with a clear pattern in color on white ground. Also a name given to a Bohemian import.

Cranberry—A beautiful wine-red glass used alone or in combination with clear glass for tableware, lamp globes, etc. Very easy to confuse with recent English importations.

Cut Glass—Any glass heavily cut with a wheel, but the term is usually used for a modern glass of the 1890s and 1900s. It is coming back into favor. Showy glass, heavy and brilliant.

Window Glass—Old window glass panes are valuable, especially the old "bubbly" glass or the amethyst panes that have been purpled from long years in the sun. Bull's-eye panes are not too easy to find but make fine bits to set in for over-door lights.

Candy Containers—The little toy containers for candies in the shapes of locomotives, lanterns, suitcases, etc. Collectors are looking for them.

Also the small glass mugs used to dip a penny's worth of candy from the jar.

Seine Balls—Glass balls of various sizes and colors used as floats on fishing seines in some localities. Also *Ball Stoppers* used to set in the mouth of jars and bottles in place of lids or corks.

Carnival Glass—A cheap and late form of iridescent glass made from 1910 to 1920. A giveaway glass in many colors, notably orange and amethyst shadings. Also called *Taffeta* Glass, *Poor Man's Tiffany*, or *Lustered*.

Rose Bowls—Very popular. Round, small-necked bowls in all the later glass styles, often with a ruffled collar.

7. CHINA AND POTTERY

IF YOU start out to look for a quantity of antique porcelain made in America you are going to be disappointed. In the early days of the colonies only common redware for utilitarian purposes was made and very little, if any, of that exists. Everything in the fine china line in the colonies was imported, much of it from England but with all Europe contributing. But this early china was so absorbed into the life of America that it must be examined briefly because old pieces that have been around for 200 years are still turning up and are not to be confused with what has just come in on the last boat from England. Besides, this is the china that was made expressly for American exportation, all the Chinese export porcelain, the Canton, Staffordshire Historic Blue, Liverpool pitchers, Gaudy Dutch and Gaudy Welsh, old ironstone, and many more. These certainly have a right to be included in a survey of American china.

A Liverpool pitcher.

When the colonists came over from England they undoubtedly brought with them the glazed redware that was in use then including slipware and scraffito more familiar to us as Pennsylvania Dutch. They also brought over a gray stoneware, salt glazed, of English use but of German origin, and this, too, was taken up by American potters in Pennsylvania, New England, New York, New Jersey, and Ohio.

Sent over but never made here was Delftware, both the Holland Delft and the English Delft, a tin-glazed ware with the designs painted on the clay before firing. Delft was the first English china to be painted. I have seen sets of Delft plates made to order for some American families dated 1738 each with the family initials. Much Delft was done in blue, but there was some polychrome.

A Delft brick.

Porcelain did not appear in England until later in the 1700s. When it did, it was not "true" porcelain like the Chinese ware it tried to imitate. Hard-paste porcelain requires kaolin, called china clay, and this was not discovered in England until 1770, when deposits in Cornwall were tapped. Thus all fine English porcelains the affluent American home imported—Chelsea, Bow, Derby, and Worcester—were of a soft-paste or "artificial" porcelain made from a white clay mixed with powdered glass. This varied considerably. On the continent, however, true porcelain was experimented with by a man named Boettger at the Meissen factory near Dresden as early as 1709.

Wedgwood brought out some fine stoneware around 1763, which differs from porcelain in not being translucent, his famous *Cream-ware* or *Queensware* as well as his jasper, basalt, and luster. The first bone china, a hard and finer type of china, was the result of experiments of Josiah Spode II who in the 1790s added the ash of burned cattle bones to a hard porcelain clay.

Wedgwood jasper teapots and creamware bowl.

China, too, sent over its blue and white Canton, forerunner of the willow pattern and what is known as Chinese Export China often misnamed Oriental Lowestoft. This beautiful ware reached America in great quantity, and in spite of much current interest is still available. Many dealers specialize in it. It has the characteristic feeling of Chinese porcelain, hard, light in weight, the glaze fused with the hard-paste base. If a piece has a glaze on the back, it was made before 1723. The "orange peel" or slight pebbly glaze is typical. It was designed in China to catch the mode and fancy of the country to which it was sent. Here in America the pieces were often decorated with the coats of arms of the colonies or states. Other pieces showed mythological subjects, patriotic motifs like the American eagle, flowers and fruits in *chinoiserie* style. It is very popular and very expensive.

Left, a Canton platter. *Right,* a willow plate.

All early patterned china was painted until about 1750, when a method of printing on china was discovered. It was called transfer printing and was done by first printing a thin paper from a copper-plate picture and then transferring it to the china piece. This transfer process did much to make china manufacture cheaper and accounts for a great quantity of the wares that were sent over to America for middle-class homes. Much Staffordshire china was transfer-printed, bearing names of famous potters from Staffordshire County in England, Enoch Wood, Ridgeway, Clews, Copeland, and so on.

In America only one experiment in early porcelain making came to anything of consequence, and that did not last long. It was Tucker China made by Tucker and Hemphill in Philadelphia from 1825 to 1838 from kaolin found in nearby Chester County. The firm ran into financial difficulties, changed hands several times, and finally folded, but in the short period of its existence it put out some fine china comparable to the French imports it aimed to copy. Much of it was left unsigned for this reason. Sepia scenes and figures, bright birds and flowers in the French manner, gold "weddingband" china characterized this ware. Not too much of it is around, although private homes in the vicinity of Philadelphia still come up with it.

By the middle of the 1800s America was producing much pottery, but the finer wares still came from abroad. Besides the output from the English factories there was Meissen from Germany, Belleek from Ireland, Sèvres and Haviland from France. This latter was produced in quantity for the American market. It was probably your mother's wedding china and she probably called it Limoges from the town in France where it was made. There is much current interest in Haviland and its patterns and it is not hard to find.

Here is some of the china you are going to hear most about and possibly find in your homes or set out to buy:

Staffordshire Historic Blue

This china came over to America in the early 1800s. It was transfer-printed and it was mostly blue, although some was printed in black, red, and later in sepia, mulberry, green, or pink. But the early blue holds more interest for the collector, especially the light blue. Much of it was made in Flow Blue or Flowing Blue, that smudged-looking china which was the result of running the color in firing to give the piece a soft, over-all coloring. It was made about 1825 and is much sought after, and many Oriental patterns like Scinde, Chen-Si, Formosa, as well as English scenes and gardens in both blue and Flowing Brown are being collected.

A Historic Blue "Fairmount near Philadelphia" platter.

The historical or commemorative china was made from about 1784 well into the 1800s. While much of it was left at home in England, it was aimed to fill the demand of the rapidly growing republic. It flattered America with a whole series of patriotic and scenic subjects calculated to warm the hearts of the people. It emphasized liberty and recorded American naval and land victories. It depicted scenes of the natural beauties of the new nation, such as Niagara Falls, and used portraits of its famous people. It put on record pictures of famous buildings and the beginnings of transportation. It did for America of the early 1800s what Currier and Ives did at a later date with their prints.

More than 200 subjects in blue Staffordshire have been listed with names of makers that include Stubbs, Enoch Wood, Adams, Jackson, Stevenson, Clews, Ridgeway, Tams, Mayer, and Green among others. Unfortunately not all of this china is marked, but those familiar with it can often recognize a maker from distinguishing patterns and borders.

There are still pieces of Historic Blue to be picked up. Just recently I heard of five different people who have unearthed plates of the landing of Lafayette, a favorite subject. Even commemorative pieces of later date have value, and there is much recent traffic in Wedgwood Blue plates of American views made from 1895 to 1910.

Another Staffordshire import is *Spatter Ware*. This is a soft-paste ware made in Tunstall, England, and sent over to America from 1845 to 1850. It can be found mostly in Ohio, Maryland, New England, and among the Pennsylvania Dutch. Occasionally a marked piece like Adams will show up. To get the mottled effect, a piece was given a spattering of color around the edges with a sponge before firing. Center designs might be a peafowl, tulip, castle or fort, cock's comb or thistle, windmill, cannon, deer, sailboat, beehive, bluebell, rainbow, or a house, probably a schoolhouse. Plaids and daubs are less desirable. Yellow is the rarest color in this ware, green the next rarest. Old spatter ware will show the triangular kiln marks. It is very primitive and often quite charming but not cheap.

Mocha Ware was another Staffordshire output that reached America. It is a type of china similar to Leeds and was made at Leeds though it is ascribed to Adams in 1787. Later it was made in Swansea and Llanelly in Wales. It is another soft-paste porcelain normally cream or café au lait in color with contrasting bands of blue, tan, or terra cotta on which designs of trees, seaweed, worms, etc., were applied in black or white.

Tiles

Tiles were used in American houses up to 1800, usually as a frame for the fireplace opening. They came from Holland and Liverpool and were Delft with a high glaze. Subjects were varied and colorful. A set of *Aesop's Fables* tiles goes back to 1760. Other pictures included rural scenes and lovers reminiscent of Watteau, biblical scenes, ships, sea monsters, children at play, soldiers, animals, flowers, and coats of arms. Colors were mostly blue and white or purple and white. Few were marked. When old houses are demolished, these tiles from around the fireplaces are salvaged for the antique market. You may find a few.

Gaudy China

This term includes several kinds of china. The best known is probably *Gaudy Dutch,* so called not because it was made for the Pennsylvania Dutch who did take it to their hearts but because of its similarity to the Oriental china brought into England by the Dutch East India Company. It was made by Staffordshire potters to copy the more luxurious porcelains of the period, the bright, gay Imari patterns of Worcester and Derby and other fine wares. Imari was Japanese not Chinese, although the Chinese copied it and often turned out finer pieces than the originals. True Imari was inspired by the brocades of old Japan and used the heraldic badges of the mandarins as well as the conventionalized chrysanthemum and other symbols all done in deep rich blues and reds and gold. Some true Imari found its way into American homes at the turn of this century, when it could be bought at popular prices.

Left, a Gaudy Dutch plate. **Right,** an Imari jardiniere.

Gaudy Dutch is the oldest china made in England for the American market. Colors are bright, rust-red and cobalt blue predominating, with touches of green and yellow. Often there is a reddish-brown rim to the plates. Usually the design centers around a single flower like a Chinese peony, but called a rose or carnation or sunflower. Fifteen known patterns include names like War Bonnet, Urn, Oyster, Butterfly, Double Rose, Dahlia, Zinnia, Dove, Grape, Primrose, and Strawberry. Prices are astronomical because it has been avidly collected.

The pattern called King's Rose is not, strictly speaking, Gaudy

Dutch but Roseware, more delicate and less boldly colored but often combining the same designs and some of the gaudier borders.

Gaudy Welsh is often used interchangeably with Gaudy Dutch but it came later in the nineteenth century and is heavier and cruder although the colors are similar to the Gaudy Dutch. It often had an impressed border and was embellished with gold luster. Both these gaudy wares came in full tea sets and coffee sets with other odd pieces of tableware. Cups were handleless.

Gaudy Ironstone or *Gaudy Imari Ironstone* is still another gaudy ware made by Mason, who put out the first ironstone in England in 1813. This, too, was imported to America in the 1800s. The story here is that this china made for the middle- and lower-class English homes was rejected because it was too reminiscent of the Crown Derby porcelain used by a snobbish upper class in the days of King William. The English people were already deep in the rococo and frills of the early Victorian era. And so Imari ironstone was dumped on America. It follows the old Imari patterns more closely than the other two. Colors are deep and rich.

Luster

No luster was ever made in America. What we buy here is from England and Wales, inspired by Spanish luster imported through Liverpool. It is a china decorated or fully covered with shiny metal-

A canary mask mug, silver luster pitcher, and two copper luster pieces.

lic colors—copper, gold, and silver. The first commercial lusterware is ascribed to John Hancock, who worked in the Spode factories in 1800. Other potters quickly followed suit in Bristol, Leeds, Sunderland, Staffordshire, and Swansea in Wales. Certain articles in this ware stand out, the pink luster shells of Wedgwood, the silver-resist pitchers of Leeds, the Sunderland transfer pitcher of the Cast Iron Bridge over the River Wear, the Newcastle election mugs and jugs, the canary mask mugs, and so on. For the uninitiated it may come as a surprise that luster is not all metallic, the copper or gold or silver often forming only a small part of the decoration.

Silver luster is made from platinum, which gives more sheen than silver. You'll find an all-over silver luster called "poor man's silver" because it could easily be mistaken for sterling or Sheffield instead of china. It is older than the other lusters and was often made over the Queen Anne and Georgian silver molds. On the other hand, silver resist was only part silver, a specialty of the Leeds factory. Here the pattern was not lustered but allowed to show through in the color of the base, which was often yellow or blue.

To make gold luster, tin was added to the formula, also a bit of iron, sometimes a bit of copper. This resulted in various tones of gold and often what we call copper luster is really a gold luster. Depending on the ground color of the piece, gold often turned out pink or purple or "moonlight," a paler purple. Copper luster was the result of a copper formula or a copper-heightened formula.

While pitchers form the bulk of the luster pieces, many other things were made, all kinds of tableware, whole tea sets, goblets, ornamental figures, Toby jugs, satyr mugs, harlequin mugs, frog mugs, puzzle jugs for unwary drinkers, tankards, jardinières, bough holders, five-fingered flower vases, knife rests, support for legs of furniture, purple cow creamers, wall plaques, and lustered pictures with biblical scenes.

Lusterware is still being made, and many of the old pieces are being honestly reproduced. Good old luster made before 1850 is smooth and clear of bubbles. It is also surprisingly light and thin. Good luster comes high.

Ironstone

Here we come to a classification that has almost as many patterns as you find in pressed glass, because ironstone is not all white as so many think who remember only the common everyday china of our grandmothers' day. Ironstone, as has been said before, was first made in England in 1813 by Miles Mason, who took out a patent for a stoneware containing powdered slag which made it less likely to chip or break and which took a white glaze that in turn took decoration as well as the porcelain it replaced. It was called variously by Mason and the other potters who adopted it semi-porcelain, graniteware, Parisian granite, and Royal Stoneware. Many of the old patterns from such makers as Adams, Spode, Minton, Ridgeway, et al., were transferred to ironstone, and you can find a galaxy of decorations that range from the classic Canton and Willow patterns up to the Tea Leaf of the 1890s.

One pattern deserves special attention, the Willow, because from its inception about 1772 by an English potter, Thomas Turner, through all its variations to the five-and-ten-cent-store counters, it has graced the American dinner table. The Willow pattern was used on Spode as well as on Minton. The first American Willow was made in Ohio about 1880. It is found in light blue and dark blue, occasionally in pink or green, and sometimes combined with gold or luster. It was the outgrowth of the Canton patterns brought over from China. It tells a Chinese legend of two escaping lovers who were turned into doves. The pattern varies considerably with the makers. Whole dinner sets were made of it as well as many odd pieces. It is not always marked. However, experts can often spot the maker by the variation in the pattern.

Other well-known patterns in ironstone are the Washington Vase, the Agricultural Vase, Blanket-stitch, Indian Tree, Spode's Tower, Wheat (Ceres), Tea Leaf, Paragon, Cashmere, Moss Rose, Grape, Athens, Onion, and Marble, to name only a few. In the pure white there are dozens of familiar patterns, which range from Grape Leaf, Fruit and Leaf, Davenport, Fig, Shaw's Fuchsia, Holly, Ceres, Cable, Boote, Trent, and so on. Many are marked.

Ironstone collecting today is fun. There is still much of it around though not in all patterns. Some are better than others. Teapots are always in demand, not only for use, but for decorative purposes, because the shapes are almost universally graceful.

Majolica

Here is a favorite that you will be meeting around the shops and discovering in your closets, particularly if you happen to live in the area of eastern Pennsylvania, for a fine American majolica was made there from 1880 to 1892. It was made also in Baltimore, Trenton, Ohio, New York, and New Hampshire in the same period.

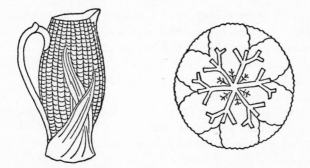

Majolica: an ear-of-corn pitcher, a shell-and-seaweed plate.

Majolica was first made in Spain and was taken to Italy in the fourteenth century. From there it moved north to France, where it was called *faïence,* and to the Low Countries, where it was known as *delft.* Such early pieces are rare and costly, mostly in museums. In England, majolica was made by Wedgwood, Minton, Copeland, and other Staffordshire potters. It came to this country in 1846, inaugurated by an English potter, Edwin Bennett, in Baltimore, Maryland. Other factories sprang up, among them the firm of Griffin, Smith and Hill in Phoenixville, Pennsylvania. Their pieces are marked GHS, with the words *Etruscan Majolica* in an oval and are otherwise identified by the orchid-pink lining of the pieces.

Majolica was a soft-paste china with a bright tin-enamel glaze. Colors were applied to the raised patterns between two firings. It chipped easily, which limits the supply of mint pieces. Patterns are fascinating, with much the feeling of English Whieldon. Of them all perhaps the shell and seaweed is the best known with the sunflower a close second. But in majolica you will find ferns, fruits, flowers, vegetables (ears of corn, cabbage heads, cauliflowers), birds,

fish, and animals, not only in the raised decorations but molded as
an integral part of the piece. Hound-handled pitchers are to be
found, also owls, parrots, swans, chicks, and ducks. Deer-and-dog
plates are prized pieces. Fans, too, were a favorite decoration as well
as shells and bamboo. Collecting a single pattern in majolica is still
possible.

Lithophanes

Because they are porcelain, lithophanes (transparencies) should
be mentioned here. They are highly translucent china plaques with
impressed pictures formed by the varying thicknesses of the china to
give light, shadows, and depth. The result when held to the light
is a fine halftone often as detailed as a fine print. They were made
to hang in windows, to shade candles, or fairy lamps, and occasionally are found in the bottoms of steins. They were made in
Germany and later in France and England. What we find today
were probably made between 1850 and 1900.

Pottery and Stoneware

One thing America did excel in, and that was its pottery of red
clay, both glazed and unglazed, and its stoneware with its salt glaze.
Much redware was brought over from England but it was soon
being made all over the colonies, especially in New York, New Jersey, Maryland, Ohio, and Pennsylvania. In Pennsylvania the German and Swiss immigrants who came to be known as Pennsylvania
Dutch took the making of redware to their hearts. Red clay was
plentiful, and it gave them a chance to indulge in the peasant
designs that were their heritage from the Old Country. Of particular
interest are the pieces in slip, sgraffito, or polychrome, the output
of many small potters. The process was an unassuming one. The
potter mixed his clay to a wet "dough" and shaped it in a block
which he kept wet for future use. From this supply he shaped the
simple utensils for home use—mugs, pitchers, bowls, plates, platters,
pie plates, vases, candlesticks, soap dishes, etc., as well as toys and
banks and pieces "for fancy," or "for pretty." He dried his pieces,
gave them a red-lead glaze, and fired them in his kiln. Any decorating was done before the glazing. For slip designs he filled a pottery

cup with a thin mixture made from white clay and poured it through one or more quills to make stripes, wavy lines, or squeeges. If he was clever, he might color his slip and build it into elaborate designs—polychrome. For sgraffito he covered the base with slip and then when it had partially hardened scratched his design through it.

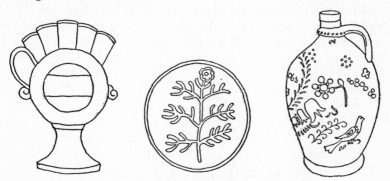

Pennsylvania Dutch pottery: a five-tubed vase, a modified "tree of life" sgraffito dish, a slip jar.

This ware has left names to be remembered from the late 1700s on: George Hubbener, David Spinner (his Lady Okie plate in sgraffito showing a lady on horseback is a classic), John Nase, Andrew Headman, Samuel Troxel, Johannes Neez, and Christian Klinker. Many of these men signed their best or "presentation" pieces, but you are not apt to find many of them left. Pennsylvania Dutch potters kept on working right through the 1800s, and later pieces are not so hard to find.

It must be remembered, too, that the Dutch moved on down from Pennsylvania through the Shenandoah Valley and we have a whole genre of both pottery and stoneware called Shenandoah Pottery from such places as Hagerstown, Maryland, Strasburg and Winchester, Virginia, and Waynesboro, Pennsylvania. It is said to compare favorably with Bennington pottery—of which more later—and added more elegance of color to both redware and stoneware.

Up in Vermont things were happening, too. Two Norton brothers moved their father's small factory to East Bennington close to some deposits of kaolin. At first the firm made only common utensils of stoneware and scroddle—a mottled ware. But later, after several various partnerships had been formed and it became the United States Pottery Company, it went in for Rockingham in a big way, from about 1841 to 1847, turning out fine Toby jugs, bottles, creamers, pitchers, mugs, teapots, inkstands, figures, plates, bowls, etc., in a mottled brown pottery with a bright glaze, glorifying the simple earthenware which originated in England and was badly copied by many potteries over here. Today you say, "A Bennington piece" in a whisper of awe and pay for it accordingly.

A Bennington hound-handled pitcher.

The stoneware turned out at Bennington under the aegis of Norton and Fenton resembles the Shenandoah pieces closely, although the latter were often decorated with more than the cobalt blue used at Bennington. This is the gray, tan, or brown ware you meet in articles such as jugs, jars, crocks, etc. Decorations are birds, flowers, and scrollwork, usually crude, but occasionally quite fine. Names and dates were also painted on the pieces. You will be lucky if you happen on a "pope's nose" jug with the scratched or modeled head of a bearded man on it, the relic of the famous Dutch Bellarmine jugs which caricatured Cardinal Bellarmino.

Among other collectible pieces in stoneware are steins. These, however, are mostly of German origin, many, and the finest, having been made at Mettlach in the Villeroy and Boch works. As these works were destroyed in 1921 by fire, Mettlach steins are at a premium. Dresden made steins, so did Wedgwood. Whatever you find will be of foreign origin, and it is well to make a study of them before making a purchase.

Figures

One of the most fascinating lanes to explore in the survey of old china is that of figures. Almost every potter of note has taken his turn at making them. Of course fine porcelains like Bow, Chelsea, Derby, and Bristol from England, Sèvres and Chantilly from France, Meissen from Germany, and perhaps the *commedia del' arte* figures from Italy, are not going to come the way of the casual buyer. But there are many that may, particularly the pottery figures from the Staffordshire factories, again many designed for the American trade. Here you find the "cottage" or mantel ornaments, things like lovers in bowers, market women, famous people such as Milton, Shakespeare, Victoria, William Tell, castles, animals, particularly the glass-eyed dogs, reclining deer, whippets, and baby lambs. They were the poor man's ornaments of around 1840 peddled from door to door. No poor man could afford them today.

Toby jugs.

Among the many English pieces imported here none are more tempting than the *Toby jugs*. There were, of course, American Tobies, too. The first Tobies were made in England in the eighteenth century. The name is supposed to have come from a character named Toby Fillpot made famous in the song, "Little Brown Jug." In fact, Tobies were often called Fillpots. The earliest figures were everyday types of imbibers, the fat man, jolly good fellow, post boy, Falstaff, etc. Later real people were portrayed in these character mugs such as George II, Lord Howe, and later Dickens, Gladstone, Nelson, Napoleon, Wellington, and Benjamin Franklin. This use of real people for Tobies has gone on up to Pope Leo XIII, Theodore Roosevelt, General MacArthur, and Winston Churchill. A Toby collector will not spurn the modern ones, especially if marked Spode or Royal Doulton, but it is the old ones that bring the prices.

Most of the English potters turned out Tobies, but the ones found most often are Doulton, Rockingham, Delft, or from the Staffordshire potteries. In size they run from one inch to eighteen inches. The average is ten inches. Colors are gay; glaze is usually glossy. Experts point out ways to identify the older pieces, such as clearly defined fingernails, teeth, etc.

They were not made in America until 1830 and were of Rockingham ware turned out by factories in Jersey City, Bennington, Vermont, and Philadelphia. Rare Tobies have been found as mustard pots and snuff boxes. I have seen a beautiful one in silver luster.

Another form of ornament popular in this country is the bisque figure. *Bisque* is an unglazed porcelain or earthenware, fragile but capable of being turned into exquisite figures. The best bisque was made in France in the 1700s. It was also made in England, the Derby figurines being a fine example. But much bisque was made for the American trade by the French as late as the late 1800s. This late bisque is what you are more apt to find—plump children on swings or dangling their fat little legs over the edge of the mantel shelf or piano top. All bisque figures bring a good price, but the earlier the better.

America made its own figures and ornaments, too. At Bennington many figures were turned out in Rockingham of which the popular poodle and the Cloaked Man bottle are prime examples. Bennington also made a fine *Parian* ware, an unglazed porcelain imitating marble and often called *Statuary* Ware. True Parian is uncolored, but at Bennington color was often applied to the pieces or added to the slip before molding. Some of the best pieces look much like Wedgwood jasper ware.

Parian pieces include cornucopia vases, Victorian hands, swans, wheat sheafs, as well as characters such as Red Riding Hood, Jenny

Lind, Queen Victoria, Washington—and again the poodles. Many other American factories in New England, Pennsylvania, New York, New Jersey, and Ohio made this ware. Some Parian is very fine, but as it is a Victorian ware much of it is overembellished to the point of bad taste.

A Parian figure and a chalkware bird.

There is another type of American ornament not to be confused with Parian called *Chalkware*. It was not chalk but plaster of Paris. Early chalk pieces were imported from England, the work of Italian artists. In 1770 a Boston stonecutter named Geyer advertised chalk figures and they soon became distributed all over the country. Later they became the cheap peddlers' wares and enjoyed great popularity in the later 1800s. It is from the later group you will probably find the most. Some of the early pieces are quite fine, imitating the pottery pieces of the early 1800s, sometimes even cast over them. There seemed to be nothing to stop the craftsman from oiling his favorite knickknack or mantel ornament and making a mold from it to be used ad infinitum. Many of the chalk pieces, especially those in the Pennsylvania Dutch country, are crude and primitive but are eagerly sought after by collectors. Early pieces are hollow with filled bases for stability. You'll find birds, dogs, and fruit pieces among these. Also some bas-relief portraits formed in cast-chalk moldings.

One more typically American figure to consider is the *Rogers Group*. Many readers will remember this dull statuary group in their own homes. They were plaster of Paris painted a grayish tan. They were sold in the seventies, eighties, and nineties, adding not so much to the artistry of American pottery but throwing light on the Victorian way of life in this country during those years. Each one told a story and was given a title such as Weighing the Baby, the Favored Scholar, Going for the Cows, Taking the Oath, Lincoln and His Cabinet. They are being sold in the shops. They are even being collected.

8. SILVER, SHEFFIELD, PEWTER, AND BRITANNIA

IT IS not given to many of us to own even one piece of genuine early American silver. I know personally only two families where pieces have come down from the 1700s, including a Syng shaker, a sugarbowl by Von Voohis, and a Revere teapot. Usually such silver must be enjoyed by visits to the museums, but a few words about this early silver and its makers should not go amiss here.

Silvermaking flourished in this country from the late 1600s on. Goldsmithing, as it was often called, was a skilled profession and the workers here had been trained in England in many instances or apprenticed to English-trained smiths. In America there were not the strict regulations imposed upon English workers. Here it was left to the honesty and the pride of the maker to put out a sterling of .925 quality which varied little. Because silver abroad was imported mostly from Spain and expensive, it was owned only by the wealthy, who called it "plate" from the Spanish word *plata*. The source of silver in this country was Spain and South America as well as England, and often coins were melted down to supply it.

Here, as well as in England, it was a top luxury for the rich. It was like money in the bank—when there were no banks, and it was bequeathed as stocks and bonds might be today. Drinking vessels seemed to be the first consideration of the silversmiths, even in puritanical New England. Boston was the first to produce fine silver, around 1660. A generation later it was made in New York and a further generation later in Philadelphia. It is interesting to examine these early pieces, each one a masterpiece of line, exquisite execution, and that soft, satiny finish which is hard to imitate. First pieces were tankards, beakers, flagons, goblets, mugs, and caudle cups for hot spiced wine. Then came the standishes, porringers, wine tasters, lemon strainers, both standing and trencher salts, shakers or casters for sugar and spice, tea caddies, nutmeg graters, punch bowls, and of course full tea sets, some chocolate pots and a few coffeepots. All tell the story of a different and affluent way of life.

A silver caster.

Many names of the famous old smiths are familiar, but of them all Paul Revere is the best known. His Sons of Liberty bowl is a classic as is the famous standish of Philip Syng, Jr., of Philadelphia, which was used at the signing of the Declaration of Independence. John Coney, Jacob Hurd, and Jeremiah Dummer were prominent names in New England; Cornelius Kierstede, Bartholomew, LeRoux and Peter Van Dyck in New York; Johann Nys, Elias Boudinot, Sr., Joseph Richardson, and Richard Humphreys in Philadelphia.

One can trace the living habits of America through the silver designs from the simplicity of the earlier pieces to a more ornate style in the mid-1700s, then a return to classic grace in the late 1700s and early 1800s. From here on American silver grew more massive and ornate until we get to the showiest Victorian pieces perhaps even now on our sideboards.

Good silver is still obtainable if you are not looking for the museum stuff, and bargains can be picked up in the sales of big estates. Any old silver is worth saving and having repaired, burnished, or replated, even the fruit basket with the broken handle which was your mother's wedding present, the darkened cakestand, the porcelain-lined water pitcher, which all seemed old-fashioned trash not so long ago. Don't overlook the smaller pieces in the family silver drawer, the odds and ends of old spoons, the servers, ladles, sugar tongs, etc. Early sugar tongs were of the scissors type, but the spring type, like the tong belonging to my grandmother with its turkey-claw ends, is of antique value, too. You will find diagrams in some of the books showing the dates of old spoons from the early round bowls, the rattail joining of bowl to handle, to the thin "coffin" or "fiddle" shapes of a later day in what your grandmother probably called "coin" silver. Coin silver, so called because of an old practice of melting down coins for making silver pieces, was of almost the same content as sterling. *Pure coin* or *warranted pure coin* or just *warranted* was used on "solid" silver when silver plating came into production in the 1830s. Later the word *sterling* was used.

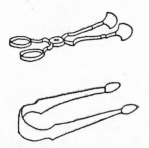

Sugar scissors and sugar tongs.

There will undoubtedly be more spoons than anything else because spoons were the sole piece of table flatware in use for a long time. Later both knives and forks were made with wood, horn, or mother-of-pearl handles until full matched sets of table silver came in. Heavy pistol-handled knives were important enough to be kept in knife boxes at the ends of the sideboards. And if you are spoon-minded don't overlook the small salt spoons, the caddy spoons, or tea skimmers, unusual things like apostle spoons, all the various kinds of souvenir spoons—a subject in itself—and the specialized spoons which graced the elegant tables of the nineties and early

1900s, the berry spoons, fish servers, pickle forks, pie servers, cake servers, asparagus forks, oyster forks, ice-cream spoons, and so on. If not antiques today, they will be in another generation. Even silver napkin rings have their use. They are being cut into wide silver bracelets and occupy the attention of collectors as well.

If you come upon a small silver box in your scavengering, handle it gently, for it may well be a patch box, a snuffbox, or a vinaigrette for fainting ladies. A silver whistle may be a true antique for whistles were used in colonial days instead of bells.

A Sheffield cake basket.

Sheffield plate was an honest endeavor to turn out a cheaper silver with a filling of copper. For years the smiths in England had been illegitimately skimping on silver by filling it with tin, but it remained for Thomas Boulsover of Sheffield in 1742 to sandwich copper between layers of silver in such a way that the effect was very close to sterling. In fact, it copied the silver of the day and was hard to recognize except by its weight, which was heavier. Sheffield to be so called was marked and had to be made with copper.

It flourished not only in Sheffield but in Birmingham, London, and France until 1840, when electroplating came in, a much cheaper process. Whereas in Sheffield the silver was fused to both sides of a copper bar, plate, or wire before it was rolled or made up into the various pieces, in electroplating silver was deposited on a copper base by a galvanic process. In America, the plating was done on a white metal base.

Practically no Sheffield was made in America. What you find will be English pieces. Much of it was marked, but the makers did not always use their marks. A few names stand out: Thomas Wallis of

London, T. and J. Crewick, Tudor and Leader for instance. But much Sheffield came to America, and it is still available though expensive. There seemed to be nothing that the workers could not do with it. There were candlesticks, many-branched candelabra, boxes of all kinds, inkstands, tea sets, tea urns, coffee sets, trays, holders for wine bottles, casters, cake and fruit baskets, tureens, egg stands, food warmers, wine coolers, salts, decanter labels, skewers, hot-water plates, lemon strainers—in fact every kind of tableware. Right here it might be well to mention the cruet stand, a popular item at the moment and available in all kinds of metal, pewter, sterling, plated silver, as well as glass and china. It is the frame that holds an assortment of bottles, shakers, and jars of condiments for the table. At its simplest it is a plated piece holding four or five simple glass bottles and jars, at its best a beautiful piece of Sheffield plate equipped with cruets and jars of Waterford glass, and perhaps supplemented with Sheffield salts and pepper shakers or a mustard pot.

An electro-plated cruet stand.

Some of the most outstanding pieces of Sheffield were in wirework. Here the copper wire was fused with a coating of silver and worked into delicately interlaced baskets and bowls or used for borders on solid pieces. An interesting piece is what is called a "potato basket," a graceful flared wire ring *not* for holding potatoes but merely a frame for a serving bowl. Wirework had the advantage of not showing the copper filling; edges of other pieces had to be rolled under or finished with a gadroon rope to hide the copper. Of course with time Sheffield will wear like any plated silver and the copper will begin to show. This is called "bloody" Sheffield. It lowers the value of a piece but purists prefer to keep it as is, a sign of age and authenticity. Replating hides the copper but destroys the whole character of the Sheffield.

Many Sheffield pieces were glass-lined—salts, sugars, mustard pots, and so on—usually with a glass of rich dark blue. Some pieces, especially the inside of bowls and cups, were gilded.

Plated silver in America began in 1847, the year when Rogers Brothers of Hartford, Connecticut, started the first successful manufacturing of the new process. Of course it did not put sterling silver out of business but it gave more people a chance to own table silver they could afford. Plated ware was marked with the maker's name and the words *triple-plated* or *quadruple-plated* as well. Later the makers of Britannia ware, like the Meriden Company of Connecticut, took to silver plating their hollow ware. In 1863 this company was the largest maker of silver plate in the country. Plated teapots and coffeepots before 1850 are apt to have wooden handles stained black to resemble ebony, and from 1850 to 1870 they had small ivory or mother-of-pearl insulators to keep the metal handles cool. With the mid-Victorian years after 1870 silver plate got almost unbearably fussy. Yet right now even such pieces are being resurrected and displayed.

There is one metal to define here—German silver. This was not silver but an alloy of copper, zinc, and nickel which came out a silvery white, another substitute but an inferior one for silver tableware. It can be electroplated if the piece seems to be worth saving.

A word about marks. The English marked their silver much more clearly and uniformly than did American silversmiths. English hallmarks seem complicated but are not hard to read if you have the code. The books of marks will tell you how. There are also books containing the marks of all the major American silvermakers, and lists with dates of the companies that made silver plate.

Pewter is an alloy of tin, antimony, lead, and copper varying in proportion according to period and maker. The best or "true" pewter has a large percentage of tin. Poor pewter has a larger percentage of lead. Britannia, a name coined by English pewterers to stimulate the use of pewter against the more general use of china in the mid-1700s, is still pewter but with a greater tin content, making it a tough, harsh-looking metal in comparison with old pewter. It is harder, thinner, and lighter in weight. Britannia was spun whereas pewter is cast. It flourished in this country during the mid-1800s. It can usually be identified by a small catalogue number stamped on the base.

The best pewter comes from the period of 1800 to 1835. Very early American pewter is hard to find because so much was melted down for bullets in the two wars. In fact, many old pieces were melted and the metal salvaged for new pewter. It was bought by peddlers who were in the habit of gathering up useless pewter to be recast into new spoons.

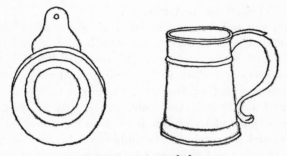

A pewter porringer and ale mug.

The quality of American pewter compared favorably with the English even though there were no compulsory laws governing its formula and markings in this country. Much American pewter is unmarked, but when the touch mark is used it is usually found on the bottom of a piece or on the inside of a hollow piece. Faint marks can often be brought out by rubbing with an ink eraser. American pewter was not overdecorated. It was simple and clean in line with only an occasional bit of engraving or "wriggling." Often the pewter and the silver of the same period are alike in shape.

Names connected with the making of pewter in America include all the Danforths, the Boardmans, and the Melvilles of New England; William Will of Philadelphia, Frederick Bassett of New York. In the forty years from 1790 to 1830 there were 75 pewterers working in the United States. Pieces with the touch marks of many of these famous names can be bought even now although a marked piece brings much more than an unmarked one.

Pewter was used for sadware, hammered over a metal plate to form platters, chargers, trays, plates, etc., and for hollow ware, molded in two or more pieces and soldered together to make cups, mugs, bowls, tankards, teapots, coffeepots, creamers, sugars, pitchers, inkwells, shakers, and so on. There were pewter spoons but no forks. Church vessels such as baptismal basins, chalices, and patens were made of pewter, and many churches today display such pieces with pride.

If you are setting out to buy pewter, don't worry if it is dark from age or lack of polish. That can be remedied. Even slightly pitted pewter is worth buying. But beware of "sick" pewter which is too corroded to answer to any treatment.

How do you polish pewter? You need, above all, plain "elbow grease" or that boon to every do-it-yourselfer, an electric buffer. If it is not bad, plain soap and water and silver polish will do the trick. Or try moistening a cloth in kerosene and dipping it in a fine kitchen scouring powder. For very bad pewter, use the finest emery powder and a very fine steel wool. Pewter can be boiled in lye, ½ cup to 1 quart of water, but it requires great caution both for the person and the pewter, and should never be done in an aluminum pot. A collector I know says he gives his pewter a yearly bath in hot sal soda water.

9. BRASS AND COPPER

AMERICA got off to a late start in making its own brass and copper pieces. One reason was the difficulty in mining and refining the copper. Another was the discouragement on the part of the English Government which wanted to keep such work at home for its own people. There were early smiths, including Paul Revere, who worked in copper as well as in pewter, tin, and of course silver. Old signed pieces have revealed the names of a few others, Molyneau and David of Boston, Noyes of Bangor, and Whittingham of New York. But as a rule you will not find much American-made brass until the late 1700s.

Not that there are not some fine old pieces of early English brass on the market, such things as beautiful bell-shaped candlesticks of "pink" English brass Queen Anne period, or finial-tipped, urn-shaped andirons of the William and Mary period, perhaps even a brass tobacco box from an old inn opening only when a coin was pressed in the slot. There is such a piece at the Raleigh Tavern in Williamsburg and I have seen one at a local dealer's. There was also Dutch brass and some French brass used in the colonies. But what concerns us most here is the American product.

Brass was used for the dials of early clocks in the English manner. Enameled dials were not imported until the 1770s. These brass dials were beautifully engraved and of course are seen mostly in the museum clocks and occasionally in a family heirloom. Brass was used also for a metal called ormolu, fashioned and gilded for an ornate trimming for clocks, frames, mirrors, and furniture in the eighteenth century. We associate it with France but it was also made in England, and appeared on American pieces.

The best American andirons were made from 1785 to 1820. From 1820 to 1850 the pieces were good but are not so desirable. Very early andirons were cast in one piece, but from 1690 to 1790 in two pieces. There were some also in bell metal, a reddish brass containing a larger percentage of copper and tin instead of zinc. Age can be judged by looking for the silver line of the seam joining the two cast pieces, often burnished to invisibility but apparent inside the piece; also by examining the screw ends of the supporting rods that show up handmade or machine-made; and by the style. You will recognize some of the features of the periods: the pad feet of Queen Anne, ball and claw of Chippendale, the tendency toward delicacy and slim shapeliness with finial tops. Knobs on thicker balusters came in the period from 1825 on.

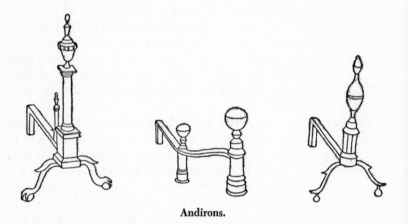

Andirons.

Fireplace tools seldom match the andirons. If you are looking for old ones, examine the iron of the shafts. The oldest will be cruder and show marks of hand forging. One thing to mention here is the jamb hook, a single or double brass hook to be screwed into the side of a fireplace to hold the tools. I lived with one for many years, not knowing what it was because it had been used as a handle on a cupboard door. Then one day a young man, an authority on old colonial metals, came along and told me I had an eighteenth-century jamb hook, and running his finger along the side of the fireplace actually found the hole where it had been originally screwed. We live and learn. Such hooks are scarce and valuable now.

Brass fenders might have been English or American. It would be hard to tell. Fine rooms had them, but not the huge open fireplaces of more primitive homes. So they were not in such extensive use here as in England where the open fireplace is still the feature in every home. They are being imported today. Naturally the finer the brasswork the better. The low serpentine rail of Adam inspiration is one to look for. You might even find a higher Chippendale fender of wirework with a brass edging.

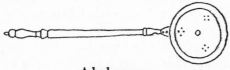

A bed warmer.

Warming pans for cold beds have always been a popular item with those interested in antiques. There is not much to do with them except hang them up at the fireplace and admire them. But they are worth admiring, especially the pierced and finely engraved ones of brass and copper. The earliest pans had iron handles but most of what you'll find now will have turned handles of walnut, applewood, ash, or oak. The brass pan might be riveted with copper or have copper banding. Warming pans are coming over from England and, while not American antiques, are often old enough and fine enough to warrant our attention. You can spot the old ones by smoke marks inside, by worn and lighter wood on the handles, worn engraving, or a loose joint between the handle and the pan.

Every fine colonial fireplace had its brass trivet—"footmen," they were called. You'll find them with cabriole legs and wooden handles, with patterns of animals and flowers, a compass or the owner's initials worked into the brass cutout design. I have seen them down South as well as in England made with hooks to hang on the fender or fire bar.

Brass candlesticks are legion, but it takes an educated eye to spot the good ones. Early candlesticks were baluster shaped with broad bases and a wide saucer to catch the dripping. In the early nineteenth century the balusters were modified and bases were often square or octagon shaped. They were made of thinly cast brass. Some had ejector rods for pushing out the candle stub. Bedroom candlesticks were saucer shaped with handles and often equipped with their own snuffers. They were made of thick sheet metal, later of cast brass. An American candlestick of Civil War days is the camp candlestick made to unscrew into several parts for easy packing. Be careful not to pay antique prices for modern Russian brass or modern interpretations of "old" candlesticks.

Some of the handsomest brass pieces to be found are the wall sconces with single, double, or even triple holders. Sconces were also parts of mirrors and were occasionally attached to furniture. Add to these the fine chandeliers, and you have covered the best of the brass. Good reproductions of all these pieces are to be had but originals are rare.

A long-handled colander.

Brass made many of the cooking utensils in the later 1700s and early 1800s. Open kettles for use on the hearth were of brass lined with block tin and having bail handles of iron. The milking kettles of a later date are similar and still in use in the Pennsylvania Dutch country if an antique dealer hasn't spotted them. Here you will find the copper apple-butter kettle, a huge affair for use over an outdoor fire. Apple-butter kettles have been avidly bought up for log holders for the fireplace. Battered and black though they may be, they come up beautifully when cleaned and burnished.

All kinds of basins, pans, and measuring mugs were made of both brass and copper as well as long-handled spoons, ladles, and skimmers. Handles often have rattail ends, and the condition of the iron will give you an idea of the age of the piece. One kitchen utensil of brass stands out in my notes, a colander with a long brass handle and a sort of horseshoe bracing of the handle at the pan. The quality of the brass, satiny from much cleaning, made it a piece to be long remembered. I would have liked to have owned it.

Probably one of the most popular items in brass or copper is the teakettle. Old ones can be recognized by the dovetailed joints overlapping at the side seams and where the bottom meets the sides. These have swan spouts and handles of iron or copper either flat or rounded. When a smith signed a kettle, he usually put the name on the handle. Some of the names to look for are Frederick Steinmetz, Benjamin Harbeson, William Bailey, and Peacock Bigger. Kettles made from 1875 on have folded seams and the bottom is pinched on to the sides.

Furniture brasses require study. You are not likely to go out buying brasses unless you have something to put them on, and if you already have them they will probably be on the piece they were designed for. But if you have any dealings with old furniture it would pay to be enlightened about what brasses go with what.

Furniture brasses.

You'll find whole chapters on this subject in the furniture books, showing with pictures and diagrams the correct brasses for the various furniture periods. Thus you will learn to recognize the teardrop pulls of the William and Mary period and the early Queen Anne, the scrolled and beveled escutcheons and bail handles that followed from 1750 on, the more ornate ones of Chippendale, the round, oval, octagonal, or lozenge-shape escutcheon plates of Hepplewhite, and the rosettes and rings of Sheraton. Furniture brasses can be deceiving, old ones often being used on later pieces to suggest an earlier date, or late ones erroneously replacing original old ones. It is seldom that you will find all the original brasses on a piece, and you have a right to be suspicious when the claim is made, because over the years the handles and escutcheons are often broken or lost. If you have doubts, look for the marks of a different plate under or around the present one, or look inside the drawers for old plugged-up holes from the screws.

There are many fine reproductions being made for all kinds of furniture brasses—handles, keyhole escutcheons, casters, and so on, and they are faithful in following period styles. If I were restoring an old piece I would rather have the right brasses even if reproduced than wrong ones.

Door Knockers

Early door knockers in this country went to the Old World for inspiration, to Spain and to Italy for the more ornate ones, and to England for the simpler ones of the Georgian era. You'll find far

A nineteenth-century door knocker.

more of the last named because in the eighteenth century and even part of the nineteenth century, before doorbells came into use, every house had its knocker, or "rapper," as it was called. Old knocker plates show great variety. Many were urn-shaped, lyre-shaped, lozenge-shaped, or oval; some were wrought with the heads of Diana, Medusa, or Ariadne. There were lions' heads, clenched fists, and women's hands holding a ball. The American eagle was a favorite of the early 1800s. Of course these are all reproduced now, but the glow of fine, old, much-polished brass is greatly to be desired if you can find it.

Bells

Here is an interesting chapter in the brass story. I am not going to talk about bells for collectors who are legion and who do not necessarily stop at old bells. What I want to point out is that there are some fine old brass bells of all kinds still in hiding and still to be found in the shops, and that they are desirable and usable today. Let's consider first the sleigh bells, so popular now that a fine string may cost as much as $1 a bell. It is interesting to know that a whole town in Connecticut, called East Hampton, is given over to the making of bells, the first factory having been opened in 1808 by a William Barton for the purpose of making hand bells and sleigh bells. He was the first to cast sleigh bells in one piece, and Barton bells were marked for three generations, W B for his own, H B for his son's, and W E B for his grandson's. The last also had a faint inscription of a horse. These are all collectibles.

Many but not all of the old makers initialed their bells. Some dated them. Marked bells are, of course, the best. Collectors who go in seriously for old bells are familiar with the many makers who flourished during the 1800s. They will tell you of E. G. Cone, who invented an acorn-shaped sleigh bell, and of another Barton who made bell toys. While the sound of the sleigh bell no longer rings out through the land sleigh bells are still made for the few hardy owners of sleighs and particularly for the American Indians, who use them for ceremonial dances.

There are many of the old bells around, full strings and parts of strings, often with the leather cracked and worn or with some bells missing. With diligence you can find old bells to match what you have, and you can have new straps made if necessary. If you happen to have a string with the bells secured with cotter pins at the back instead of rivets, you are lucky, for they are easily detached for cleaning. Don't mistake the handsome Russian bells for the home output.

Finer bells were engraved and some handsome strings are made up of bells of graduated sizes. A good string might run to forty bells. Dealers are doctoring up odd lengths to be used as doorbells—a very attractive idea, especially for the country house. I have tied a handful of odd bells together with a leather thong for the same purpose. I have also hung a single old engraved bell the size of an orange on a screen door to tinkle and give warning of a caller.

After the sleigh bells come the other horse bells, or shaft bells. Of them all the Conestoga bells are the finest. These adorned the famous six-horse bell teams that rolled out from eastern Pennsylvania toward the West, hauling freight and whole families in their "prairie schooner" wagons. For such a team there were full sets of bells, five bells each for the lead horses, four for the middle horses, and three for the rear. These bell arches are in high demand and turn up not too frequently in the shops. But when one does, hop on it! They give some of the sweetest bell music to be heard.

You can still find cowbells and sheep bells, those little Alpine-type squared bells of sheet brass or copper hung on the necks of the animals allowed to pasture unfenced. You can hear them even now in the hilly country of Vermont. Brass school bells are another popular item on the antique-shop shelves. Good ones bring good prices, especially the large ones with finely turned handles of tiger maple. Farm bells hung close to the house to call the hands to dinner were of an alloy called bell metal and not polished, but you will find other larger bells, such as ship's bells and fire engine bells, that are.

Two not-so-old but interesting bells are doorbells, one a store bell equipped with a flat metal coil that acted as a spring and caused the bell to tinkle when the store door was opened. The other is a hemispheric bell with a clapper that was attached to the inside of a house door and was pulled by a string on the outside or worked with a lever. There were brass table bells to summon the "hired girl," church bells, and a push-button bell on a marble stand for store or office. Some of these were made of other metals, too. All are worthy of respectful treatment.

Some of the many things you will find made of brass are:

Weather Vanes
Wood Boxes
Doorstops
Chafing Dishes
Inkwells
Old Locks, Keys, and Hinges
Powder Horns
Sundials
Snuffboxes or Tobacco Boxes
Trays
Buttons
Mortars and Pestles

Lamps
Clocks
Bootjacks
Cuspidors
Pie Crimpers
Mirrors and Photo Frames
Scales
Tea Caddies
Patch Boxes
Plaques
Horse Brasses

10. IRON

IRON, both the wrought iron and the later cast iron, supplies the antique business with some of the most interesting and valuable pieces. Iron mining and working were one of the earliest industries in this country. As early as 1621 there is a record of an ironworks in Virginia destroyed in an Indian raid, and in 1685, at Saugus River, near Lynn, Massachusetts, which operated only a few years. There were other sporadic attempts in the colonies to mine and smelt ore but it was left to Pennsylvania to set up the first successful forges and furnaces with the establishment of Thomas Rutter's ironworks in Berks County (near what is now Pottstown) in 1716. Shortly thereafter Samuel Nutt came over from England and took up part of a Penn grant in Chester County and opened Coventry Furnace. From then on the forges and furnaces multiplied, moving up the valley of the Schuylkill River and setting up the vanguard of the big steel industry to come.

Most of the iron mined was either bog iron from along the streams or dug from shallow mines. There was no machinery for deep mining. Today a huge industry is mining iron from those unexplored iron veins. Foreign workers were brought over—English, German, and Scotch-Irish. An old "iron plantation" was a self-sufficient community like the cotton plantations of a later day. Besides skilled labor, bond servants, Indians, and even a few slaves were used. They turned out the bar iron for forging and welding and "pigs" of more brittle iron for casting. The life of the colonies was dependent upon the pieces made at these forges, the cooking utensils, wagon-wheel rims, tools, hardware for doors and furniture, nails, and, later, the cannon and balls for the wars.

One of the most important items manufactured by the furnaces were the stoves. While the English held to their open fireplaces, the Germans liked their stoves and were responsible for the first five-plate stove, an iron box open at one end which was set into the wall of a fireplace from another room. When filled with embers, the stove heated the room that had no fireplace. Later it was improved, given a sixth side, a stovepipe, and a fuel door. Still later, about 1761, the first cooking stove was made, called a ten-plate stove.

It was 1744 when Benjamin Franklin invented his detached movable iron fireplace, designed to reflect back the heat that escaped up the huge Pennsylvania fireplaces. It was a new heating idea and he gave it outright to his old friend and patron, Robert Grace, who had married into the Nutt family and with his wife was operating both Coventry and Warwick Furnaces. Franklin's original idea was modified in many ways and manufactured by many firms. It is still made, for it is a very useful piece of heating apparatus.

Ruins of some of these old forges and furnaces and the houses of the ironmasters still remain though the industry moved on. Left behind are reminders of the old pocked iron smelted over the deep charcoal pits that denuded the woodlands of the countryside. Thus you will occasionally find not only whole stoves but single plates of them, often quite decorative. There are still to be had the decorative iron firebacks which were placed in every fireplace as protection and to throw back the heat. These were cast from wooden molds designed by German artisans and were often of biblical inspiration. Museums and interested collectors have, of course, depleted the supply of both these items to a minimum. But it is not likely that the average antique seeker will miss them.

There are, however, many other evidences of this early industry that will interest anyone who is remodeling an old house. These are the old locks, latches, and hinges. Styles vary in the different parts of the country, and it is well to stick to the old iron that was used in your locality if you can. Latches seem to vary more than other items. The thumb latches fall into two classes: Norfolk latches with a back plate and Suffolk latches with no plate. It is easy to identify the Pennsylvania Dutch pieces with their cutout hearts and tulips, but an iron expert can point to the shells and pine-tree motifs of New England, an Oriental note influenced by the China trade, or a French touch from Huguenot settlers.

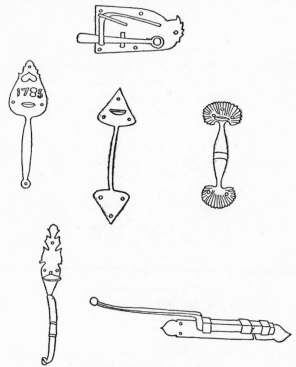

Door latches and fastenings.

Locks were usually of the box type or of oak and iron combined. A later lock and one still available is a small square lock with a thumb-press lever at the top inside and a latch handle on the outside. It locked with a key. Old keys are worth saving if only for the novelty of them. I've seen a most attractive door knocker made from a ring of old keys.

Hinges range from the plain strap style, short or long with rattail or foliated ends, through ox-shoe braced, butterfly, H and H and L, angle, frog's leg, serpentine, and many other ingenious patterns for reinforcing a swinging door or lid. Some of the finest hinges to be found are on old chests or from the lids of the Conestoga wagon boxes.

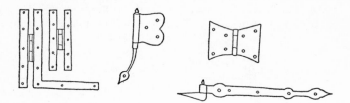

Door hinges.

Shutter hardware, bolts, hinges, and guards, should not be ignored. Nor hooks of any kind, especially the meat hooks that were hammered into cellar or attic beams to hold the smoked meats or bunches of dried vegetables out of harm's way. Save every old square-headed handmade nail you can find. It is safe to say here, never throw out an old hinge or lock or latch until you have it examined by an authority. It took an expert to tell me that some old H hinges which I had left on several of the doors in my old house were not just everyday H hinges—valuable as those may be— but early ones with foliated ends which placed them as Queen Anne period and made before 1720. Now I gaze on them with awe.

Other things in old iron to salvage or to buy when you find the price is right are:

Weather Vanes—While many were made of copper and even of wood, there were iron weather vanes, the early ones cut from sheet iron, later ones cast. A favorite in Pennsylvania was the Indian with his arrow pointing into the wind, used supposedly to reassure bands of marauding Indians. In New England there was a preponderance of ships and fish. In all localities there were cocks and other animals as well as "story" groups.

Candlesticks and Rush Holders—Early ones are rare both in floor and table brackets. Some had scissors-type or retractable arm extensions, some could be raised and lowered in a spiral tube, some had spikes for thrusting into a chimney jamb, some hung on the backs of chairs. A later iron stick is the "hog-scraper stick" with a push-up candle spring. The thin round base could be reversed with the stick for the handle for scraping bristles from scalded pigs, so it is said.

Andirons—Early ones of iron were quite simple, ending in spheres, cones, tapering ends bent back to form circles, and faceted ends. Later cast-iron andirons were vase-shaped or globe-shaped. Notable exceptions to the rule of simplicity were the Hessian soldiers (extensively reproduced), figures of Benjamin Franklin or Washington, ships, houses, or owls.

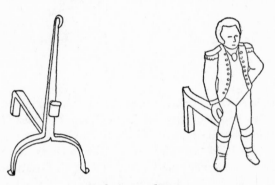

Early iron andirons.

Fireplace Equipment—Swinging *cranes* made to slip in rings in the stonework of the fireplace; *trammels,* long notched bars for hanging the cookpots at certain heights; *S hooks,* for holding the bails of the pots. Pokers, tongs, peels (flat paddles for lifting bread from the brick ovens), pipe lighters.

Cooking Utensils—All the pots and pans used in fireplace cooking, three-legged "gypsy pots," Dutch ovens, grills, toasters, waffle irons, teakettles, reflector ovens, etc. Also spoons, ladles, forks, skimmers, and skewer hooks (look for rattail handles, hearts, or tulips). Cherry seeders, pea shellers, apple parers, gem pans, lady-finger molds, waffle and wafer irons, and iron bowls.

Trivets—A favorite collector's item. The old wrought-iron trivets are more valuable. Some were equipped with tall legs for use over a fire or with a ring to hold a pot. A three-legged trivet was called a spider, a six-spoked one a cat. Smaller ones with short legs were merely used as hot plates. Sadiron stands are classed with trivets but are later, and are usually cast iron. Made from 1830 on. There are hundreds of patterns for the collector: letters, mottoes, symbols of fraternal orders, and so on. They make fine plant stands or hot plates even if you have no desire to collect them.

Trivets.

Boot Scrapers—Just as useful today as when they were made. Some are still standing at the doors of old houses. They were usually designed with two spikes or feet to be set into bricks or masonry. One type had a single spiked end to set into the masonry of the house, or was an iron arc with two spikes to set into the side of the door. Victorian ones were set into marble slabs. All are of value today.

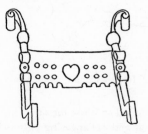

A Pennsylvania boot scraper.

Parlor Stoves—Popular from 1850 to 1880 before central heating and the first cast-iron furnace came into use in 1870. The urn stove with a vase humidifier on the top was a favorite. There were also some attractive small stoves for bedrooms. Of doubtful use now, although I have seen them used in the right rooms as auxiliary heaters.

Hitching Posts—The most familiar ones are the horse's head and the jockey —both reproduced now. Older ones had ball heads or rings and chains.

Fire Marks—These are the iron plaques put on houses by the early fire-insurance companies to indicate the insured houses and thus get preferential treatment from the fire companies. Later on they were pure advertising. Two of the earliest and most valuable are the Hand-in-Hand and the Greentree (though this was lead on wood).

A Fire Association of Philadelphia fire mark, about 1817.

Bootjacks—Beetles, pistols, Naughty Lady, etc. In demand.

A folding-pistol-type bootjack.

Snowbirds—Iron eagles or other birds for attaching to a roof to keep the snow from sliding off and endangering gutters or planting.

Mortars and Pestles—Although many were wood and some were brass, there were iron ones for grinding spices, etc.

Fluting Irons—For ironing frills and ruffles. Oldest was an iron-handled tube like a curling iron in a three-legged stand. There was a roller type, too, with ridges that rolled over a ridged stand to flute the muslin.

Sadirons—All the old handled types that were heated on a wood or coal stove. Used today for doorstops or book ends.

Branding Irons—People are turning these into candlesticks.

Doorstops—Heavy iron figures, usually animals and often painted.

Plant Stands and Brackets—Both the swinging-arm kind and the tiered stand are popular for house plants. Some people paint them white. These are being reproduced, too.

Match Safes—The wall type, single and double safes, provide enough variety to get the collectors excited.

A Victorian wall match box and twine holder.

Twine Holders—Round or beehive-shaped, from old stores. Usable for the home.

Bill Holders—Those spiked brackets or standing files. Still good for their original purpose.

Scales—Those with the brass scoops more desirable.

A Fairbanks scale, about 1830.

Lawn Ornaments—Urns, animals, etc. Some people want them.

Lawn Furniture—The lacy kind of chairs, settees, and tables is very usable for terraces and sun porches. Extensively reproduced.

Wirework—Baskets, plant stands, etc. Can be most attractive.

Some of these iron things you would not set out to buy unless you could see a direct use for a certain piece, but with kitchens going Early American, fireplaces still popular inside the house and outside, many old iron things have legitimate uses. There are still interesting iron items lying around unappreciated in old houses, and if you are not inclined to keep them they all have a ready sale value of some kind.

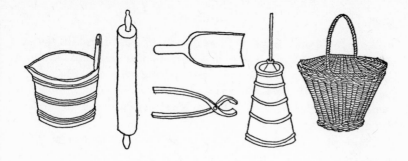

11. KITCHEN STUFF

FROM the kitchens of our pioneers have come some of the most interesting pieces in the story of antiques. Here is all the fascinating woodenware, tin, basketry, stoneware, etc., much of it the product of local craftsmen. In other words, primitives, folk art. Even the not-so-old pieces from Victorian pantries and kitchen have value as relics of a different way of life, and many an amusing or even useful utensil made up to 1900 can be worth the buying or saving.

Woodenware

Wooden implements for the home go far back in our history because wood of all kinds was the most available material and was easily worked with simple tools. In England, old woodenware is called *treenware,* and Tunbridge was a center for it. In this country much early woodenware was brought over from England at least until the mid-1700s, when it became a thriving business in New Hampshire, Vermont, and Massachusetts. In the 1800s Winchendon, Massachusetts, became the woodenware center of the world. The Shakers of New York and New Hampshire made fine wooden utensils from the late 1700s to the mid-1800s. Of special interest are the hair sieves and pantry and herb boxes of pine with maple riveted bands.

Early woodenware was fashioned by hand, and it is said that the Indians showed the colonists how to make hollow ware. However, lathes soon began to take the place of handwork. By 1820, when a lathe for turning gunstocks was invented, woodenware no longer depended upon the whittler, although his clever knife kept on working for many years.

Those who shaped the wooden pieces were called turners. There were coopers, too, "dry" coopers who made staved and bound buckets and measures for grains and dry materials, and "tight" coopers who made the watertight pieces with bands of iron or copper—kegs, barrels, churns, tubs, etc., usually of white oak.

Burl pieces were the choicest of all. They were made from the knotty growth of hard- or semi-hard woods like walnut, maple, ash, mahogany, or birch. They were usually shaped by hand and resulted in pieces with beautiful markings. A good burl piece today is a find.

There is no hard-and-fast rule for telling the age of old woodenware for it is seldom marked. Of course the more primitive pieces are self-evident. However, if the marks of old tools are evident, if edges are worn, if there are stains and scratches, if there are wooden pegs or handmade nails, if staves are smooth and well finished, if the piece is light in weight, and if you can detect the patina of age you probably have an old piece.

Things to look for:

Old Eating Utensils—Plates, trenchers, mugs, salts, tankards, spoons, forks —all rare but still to be found.

Molds—*Marchpane* or *marzipan* molds are all collectors' items. Used by the sugar bakers of Europe (especially Belgium) for shaping the sweetmeats made from pounded almonds and sugar. They were used and a few made over here and occasionally you will find a ceremonial mold carved for a special occasion.

Springerle Boards are similar to the marzipan carved boards. They were used for the Swiss and German Christmas cookies. Whole collections have been made of these which were designed in squares to take care of from six to twenty-four cookies at one pressing. A different figure appears on each square—a goat, pagoda, bird, girl, house, fruit, flowers, etc. The carving is very sharp, the wood fine grained, probably holly. *Springerle Rolling Pins* were carved from maple with designs for about sixteen cookies. These date from about 1850. There are modern ones made today.

Butter Molds are of great interest to the collector. While they are associated with the Pennsylvania Dutch, who made many fine specimens, they were used all over the country in dairying areas. Designs are numerous and beautiful. Familiar ones are: cow, tulip, heart, eagle, star, swan, hen, dove, sheaf of wheat, acorn, pine cone, pineapple,

Butter molds. *Left to right:* **tulip design, eagle design, heart design.**

A marzipan mold.

Prince of Wales feathers. Often the initials of the farmer were cut into the design. There was a rectangular trough print for stamping out the one-pound brick as well as the smaller round one for the butter pat. Occasionally a round mold will have two sizes of prints in one piece, a different design for each. *Bag Stamps* are often confused with the butter mold. These were wood blocks for stamping a farmer's name or insignia on his homespun grain sacks. Early molds were hand-carved and show more originality. Later ones were lathe turned.

Spice Chests—Some of these were very fine pieces of furniture and were not kept in the kitchen at all. They followed the furniture styles of the various periods. But there were many others, small hanging pieces, tiers of drawers for spices sometimes combined with small salt or sugar bins. They were in use over the whole country and make good finds today for kitchen *décor* or for other purposes. Greatly copied for gift shops.

A walnut spice cabinet.

Spoon Racks—A hanging piece consisting of a carved or cutout board with notched shelves for displaying the precious spoons. Rare and early.

Tea Caddies—Tea caddies (from the word *kati* or *catty,* a measure) were made of many things besides wood—pewter, silver, Sheffield, tortoise, lacquer, mother-of-pearl, enamel, tin, shagreen, etc. Wooden caddies were of various kinds, boxes and chests in styles of the period furniture makers with two inside compartments for two kinds of tea with perhaps a Waterford glass slop bowl and a silver skimmer included. One of the most interesting of the wooden caddies is that shaped like a large fruit, an apple perhaps or a pear, and made, possibly, in fruit wood.

Candle Boxes—Very desirable, especially the decorated ones. These boxes are long and narrow, about twelve by five inches with a sliding lid.

Knife Boxes or Trays—A divided tray box with handle for holding the table silver, sometimes with lid. Usually quite simple and made from pine, although you may find a fine walnut piece with inlay. Very nice to have; usable for many things.

Hanging Racks and Wall Boxes—All kinds of salt boxes and dredgers, of all wood or combined with crockery. Also pipe racks, comb cases, and other unidentified cases. Sometimes carved. Add to these the expandable hanging wall racks for newspapers and magazines with little white buttons at the intersections of the crisscrossed pieces. Also hatracks.

Dough Boxes—Oblong boxes with or without legs but with lids for holding the rising dough. They are being used for many things, those with legs being turned into low end tables. An unusual dough box in a collection is round with a lid and is painted in the old red paint.

Bowls—Of every shape and form, mixing bowls, milk bowls, and many others turned from a single piece of wood. Oblong and trough shapes are very desirable. They can be used as is for salad bowls, or cleaned, oiled, and finished like any piece of pine or maple furniture for use as work baskets, magazine stands, etc.

Pails and Measures—These make surprisingly good-looking wood and log holders for the fireside. Also scrap baskets. Look for staved and banded grain measures, maple-sap buckets, etc. *Handled Measures* in sets can be effectively used for flower holders and planters or for pure ornament.

Lehnware—Wooden utensils and knickknacks made from 1860 to 1890 by Joseph Lehn of Lititz, Pennsylvania. This is a naïve painted woodenware using the gaudy designs of the "queensware" in gay colors on dull pink or yellow grounds. Distinguished by the pussy-willow borders. Pieces included goblets and cups, notably saffron cups with lids, egg cups, spice cabinets, vases, washbasins, little drawered cabinets for seeds, lidded sugar tubs for table use, and footed trinket chests. Rather recently taken up by collectors.

Lehnware pieces.

Carved Ornaments—Not strictly kitchen pieces, but they should be mentioned because hand-carved. Prominent are the Schimmel eagles made by an itinerant whittler, Wilhelm Schimmel, who roamed the Cumberland Valley of Pennsylvania in the latter half of the 1800s. He made many toys and ornaments of which his piece, the Garden of Eden, is a classic. There were other carvers of note throughout the country. In New England it is the Bellamy eagle that is talked about.

Bellows—Plain, beautifully carved or painted and lacquered. With brass tips and fine leatherwork.

Mortars and Pestles—Large ones for grain and corn, smaller ones for salt, sugar, spice, and herbs. Fine ones were of burl, lignum vitae, Quassia wood, or bird's-eye maple. Simpler ones of pine. Many in brass or iron.

Coffee Mills—Of many styles from the kind with a wheel or wheels used in the stores to the wall type or the square box with a drawer that you held in your lap. All popular.

Bread or *Baking Boards*—Even these can be attractive when differently shaped or with a cutout handhold in heart or other pattern.

Rolling Pins—Besides the springerle rollers there were other patterned ones, one with a spiral for working the butter, crude homemade ones of hickory, or fine finished ones of walnut. Make interesting kitchen pieces.

Potato Mashers—You can still use these home-whittled mashers if you don't have an electric mixer. Handy.

Pie Crimpers—Those little crimped wheels for finishing pie edges.

Pie Lifters—Two-pronged wooden tool for taking hot pie out of oven.

Wooden Peel—Long-handled flat shovel for removing bread from brick oven.

Cabbage Cutter—A Pennsylvania Dutch piece for shredding cabbage for coleslaw or sauerkraut.

Cranberry Picker—Plentiful in New England. They are being turned into magazine racks.

Washboards—Primitive ones had china rollers, or were two separate ribbed boards to be rubbed together. Can't imagine anyone but a collector of Americana wanting these.

Scoops—For cream, soap, meal, flour, sugar, etc., often with a hooked end to hang on a bowl.

Quassia Cup—A small wooden cup made from quassia wood which imparted a bitter taste to water, making it "medicinal."

Sticks—Toddy sticks, dye sticks, maple-sugar stirrers, apple-butter paddles, feather-bed smoothers, dough paddles, and doughnut lifters.

Butter Paddles—Make wonderful servers for nuts, popcorn, etc.

Dippers—For water, milk, etc.

Hair Sieves or Temses—Of interest to collectors.

Cheese Presses

Shoemaker's Lasts and Hat Forms

Ox Yokes or Shoulder Yokes

Foot Stoves—With perforated tin boxes in wooden frames.

Baskets

Basketry is an ancient craft. Materials for making baskets have always been close at hand in every country, from reeds to roots, pine needles to cornhusks. The early colonists were most concerned with straw baskets, splint baskets, and willow baskets. Some of the tricks of basket weaving they learned from the Indians.

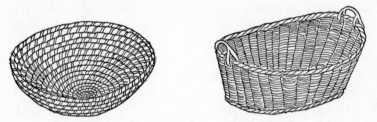

Left, a straw basket. *Right,* a wicker cradle.

For making willow baskets, the old basket makers often grew special groves of willow trees, choosing several varieties, such as the American green willow, the purple Welsh willow, or the Caspian willow. It took about five years to establish a good willow orchard. Usually one-year shoots were used for weaving. Dry or "cured" willow was soaked in water to make it pliable for weaving.

Splint baskets were made of wood stripped into ribbons or *schiens,* as the Pennsylvania Dutch called them. They had a low workbench for doing this stripping called a *schnitzelbank*—hence the old ditty, *Hast du denn ein schnitzelbank? Ya, ich hab ein schnitzelbank,* on the Hit Parade in the Dutch country. The wooden ribbons were woven into baskets. Woods used were ash, elm, willow, and the sturdy hickory. Straw baskets were made from ropes of straw held together by windings of a strong reed.

All this old basketry is still to be found. It was used for baskets for grain, cheese, for baking bread, with two-part bottoms for carrying eggs, bottle baskets, woven covers for casks and bottles, straw mats, clothes baskets, cradles, Easter baskets, workbaskets, beehives, or skeps. You'll also find other straw articles such as palm-leaf hats and starched straw bonnets sold by the peddler in the little red wagon.

Old baskets are interesting though usually not of much value in dollars and cents. If you have any, or find them, scrub them up and use them for wood, magazines, scraps, toys, knitting, etc. They are well worth salvaging.

Tin

Lucky you who have in your possession some pieces of old tin, plain, pierced, or decorated! Tinware has risen in value over the years as more and more casual collectors have become aware of it. Even the crude unpainted pieces have been snapped up for decoration and the restoration of original patterns by the many who have learned the art of painting upon tin. Not so long ago one could pick up an old coffeepot or measure or tea caddy for a few cents at a country sale. Now, it is almost impossible to find them, and if you do, you will have to pay with real folding money. But if the old painted decoration is distinct and the tin is in good condition you will have something to be proud of.

Tinware was not just a product of the late 1800s. It went much farther back, but it did not come into common use in America until after the Revolution. America had no tin and England preferred to export tin articles rather than the metal which put the sources of Welsh mines to good use. Old tin is not like today's tin. It was a sturdy product made by coating a thin layer of iron with a tin facing. The chief tinworks of Britain were at Pontypool and today you hear Pontypool pieces spoken of with great respect. However, England did export a japanned ware to this country made expressly for the American trade. Much of it still survives.

The process called japanning was inspired by Oriental lacquering whereby a piece was coated and polished over and over with a gum product until a hard, glossy surface resulted. The nearest the European could come to it was by using colorful varnishes and baking them. So what you are likely to find among the better pieces today is this japanned tin either imported from England before the 1780s or the later products made in this country and decorated by local craftsmen. You will recognize the old varnishes because the pieces have a brownish look, the black as well as the reds and mustards. In many of the handbooks on painting tin you will find formulas for getting this "antique" look. There are even "antique" paints to be bought already mixed.

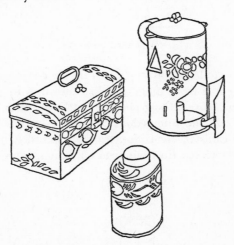

Old painted tinware. The object at right may have been used as a baby's milk warmer. There is an opening at the bottom for a small spirit lamp and a pan at the top that can be removed.

New England, notably Berlin, Connecticut, was a tin center. Pennsylvania was another. The Dutch took to tin for applying their peasant designs. The Yankee peddler in the early 1800s carried tin to the eager housewives and if it was a painted piece it was probably reserved for show rather than use. The most popular pieces were trays, lace-edged, galleried, scalloped in the Chippendale manner, octagonal, oblong, or oval with handholds. Work was mostly freehand with roses, scrolls, exotic birds, fruits, etc. combined in an easy, unstudied way. It was not until later that stenciling was used. Much bronze, gold, and other metallic powders were combined with the gesso and oil colors. Pontypool trays are distinguished by clever use of line borders.

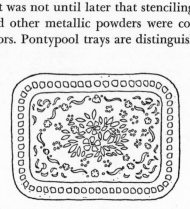

A painted tin tray.

Other pieces to be found in painted tin are coffeepots, tea caddies, bread trays, apple trays, mugs, handled measures in gills to quarts, syrup pitchers, covered sugarbowls, bottle warmers, boxes of all kinds, especially the humped-lid document boxes. Also desirable are the store canisters for coffee, tea, and spices. A new collectible is the transfer-printed tin from 1900 on, plates, canisters, trays, etc.

Cookie cutters.

All old tin you find will not be painted, however. It may be pierced in design, or crimped around the edge, or stamped like an old ABC plate. There is a mellowness about old tin that is almost as pleasing as pewter. One thing in particular in plain tin has become a very popular item for collecting—*cookie cutters*. Here the tinsmith really went to town to please the housewife. Every household had its collection, some very personal and unique. There was always a set of angels, trees, stockings, Santas, etc., for the Christmas cookies, which were frosted and used for tree ornaments. But you'll also find many other things when you start looking, such as eagles, hearts, tulips, daisies, boots, men and women, horses, lambs, dogs, pipes, and violins. One of the uses for the cutter was for gingerbread introduced into Pennsylvania by the Germans. The gingerbread maker was an important man as witness one Christopher Ludwig who became Baker General for the Colonial Army and was honored by Washington. Many towns had their bakers who cut their dough into elaborate cakes shaped like soldiers, horses, men on horseback, men, women, and animals.

Stoneware and Pottery

When Grandmother set her newly churned butter in a stone crock for storage in the springhouse or put down pickles in a big jar or poured cider from a stone jug she never dreamed that someday her granddaughter would be showing off these humble household stand-bys as antiques and giving them new uses in her modern home. There is much of this gray, tan, cream, and brown stoneware around,

Stoneware jugs. *Left*, a Selenus jug with monk's face. *Right*, an imprinted jug.

What you will find is American made in the nineteenth century, and was discussed briefly in Chapter 7. However, it might be well to add a few more notes right here. Many old pieces were not marked, many were. Names to remember are Remmey of Philadelphia, Norton and Fenton of Bennington, Vermont, and Foulke of Morgantown, West Virginia, among many others which you will find listed in the pottery books.

A true collector knows what to look for in a good piece—shape, color, clear designs, and good color in decorations, the way the handle is applied, and whether it is ear shaped or ring shaped. Here are the things you will find: jugs for vinegar, molasses, cider, and rum; crocks for butter, cheese, and cream; jars for pickles and con-serves; milk pans; chambers; spittoons; bean pots; churns; water jars with spigots; flowerpots; pudding dishes; molds; bowls; pitchers; batter pitchers; bitters bottles; ginger-beer bottles; beer mugs; banks; foot warmers, and many other odd and useful articles.

Many of these pieces can be put to new use without stretching a point. Jugs and jars make fine lamp bases; crocks serve as jardinieres; almost any piece can be turned into a planter; large jars make ideal umbrella stands; and a row of pitchers, mugs, or molds will beautify any modern kitchen as well as being handy for the use for which they were intended.

Other pieces of kitchen pottery not in this stoneware class are also taking on value, things such as yellow or white glazed pudding molds, turk's heads of any kind, all kinds of mixing bowls, especially a blue-dappled ware. There is a sturdy nostalgic quality about all these things that stands out among the aluminum and stainless steel in today's kitchens. Cherish them.

12. CLOCKS AND WATCHES

I F YOU own a genuine antique clock that has come down in the family you are lucky. If you are setting out to buy one, prepare to pay plenty because fine old clocks are not picked up on a bargain counter. A good old clock, especially what we call a grandfather's clock, is an investment but not one to be entered into idly. Consult the books and learn something about what you intend to buy. Many books will have lists of American makers of clocks where you may find the name engraved or painted on the dial. The lesser-known names, of course, will not bring the prices of the big ones.

American clocks were made all through the history of the colonies by men who learned their trade from English clockmakers. The first clocks were apt to be clocks for public buildings and church steeples. In the homes hourglasses were used as late as 1812. But long before that date some of our most famous clockmakers started working and what they turned out was the pendulum clock which was either a "hang-up" type or enclosed in a tall wooden case.

The hang-up clock was what we call the wag-on-the-wall, just the works, face, and pendulum. There are still some around. It was the way clocks were delivered to customers who were supposed to supply their own tall cases—and perhaps didn't. Cases were more often made by the furniture makers than by the clock men, and sometimes by the home or local craftsmen. But some of the finest specimens of early cabinetmaking of the 1700s are found in the cases of the tall clocks. Tall or long-case clocks were made by most of the

American clockmakers from 1680 to 1840, particularly in New England, New York, New Jersey, Pennsylvania, Maryland, Virginia, West Virginia, Ohio, and eastern Kentucky. These are the regions where you will be most likely to find the old ones even now.

They copied the fine old English tall clocks of the periods and you will find engraved brass dials (imported), brass works made in America, illuminated arches above the dial with rocking ships and moving phases of the moon, the best lines of Chippendale and other English furniture makers, and pendulums that beat the seconds. They were eight-day clocks.

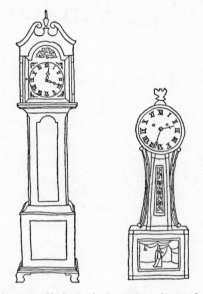

Left, a grandfather's clock. *Right,* a banjo clock.

Later on a shorter pendulum was used to beat the half seconds and up to 1807 wooden works were made for such clocks. They were thirty-hour clocks. It was Eli Terry of Connecticut who fathered the shelf clock with the shorter pendulum. He is famous for his pillar-and-scroll clock-case, a style which with many variations went on for twenty-five years. A few other names in this period were Elias Ingraham, who made wall clocks in classic designs called Gothic, Doric, Ionic, etc.; Seth Thomas, who for a time was in partnership with Hoadley and Terry; Simon Willard, who made the famous banjo clock, as well as other clocks; David Rittenhouse in Philadelphia; Christopher Sower (who spelled his name Souers on his tall clock); and a man named Edward Duffield, a friend of Benjamin Franklin, also of Philadelphia, who made a double-face clock for display purposes.

The story of old clocks makes interesting reading. We learn that there was no such thing as a "grandmother's" clock. The name was picked up probably because it was a short clock and could be wound by a woman with ease. It was called a miniature tall clock or a dwarf tall clock and a half-clock, not because it was half the height of a tall clock (4 feet against 7½ or 8 feet), but because the makers in numbering their clocks often gave it a half number. Tall clocks were made from about 1750 to 1850.

Other clocks you will see and hear of:

Mantel Clock—Name for any clock including the "shelf clock" that does not stand on the floor or hang on the wall.

Bracket Clock—A clock that fits a bracket made just for it. Usually English, Lantern Clock, Bird-cage, etc.

Lyre Clock—A form of banjo clock, lyre-shaped in the waist.

Looking-glass Clock—With a mirror in the door or panel of the door instead of the reverse painting on glass.

Lighthouse Clock—A Willard clock with a bell-glass over the works and dial and a pillared base. Rare.

Steeple Clock—Small shelf clock with steeplelike finials on the pillars and pointed top. Also a Double-steeple clock.

Chippendale Shelf Clock—With broken arch and finials at the top, painted glass door and bracket feet.

OG Clock—Designating the molding of the frame. Mantel clock made from 1848 to 1888. Also an OOG clock with double molding. Available.

Wagon-spring Clock—Shelf clock of the mid-1820s. Mechanism controlled by wagon-type spring, no weights, no coil springs. Duncan Phyfe made cases for these clocks. Collectors' items.

Bronze Mantel Clock—Late half of 1800s. Made by Ansonia and others with bronze figures. Figures alone, especially horses, have value.

This list does not include a host of novelty clocks made from time to time and enjoying a brief popularity, nor the cuckoo clock which of course was—and is—imported. An "antique" clock should be at least one hundred years old. Novelty clocks can and probably will be younger, as will the "railroad clocks," office clocks, and school clocks. If you do set out to buy a clock, try to identify it by a signature, or look inside for a clock paper. See if you can find it in the books. It might not be important enough for that but still be a good clock provided the price is right. It is far safer to buy a clock in running order. It will cost more, but the risk is less. If you buy one that needs repairing, be sure to allow a good stiff sum to add to the initial cost. There are men around who are wizards with old clocks, who can make new parts if necessary, so no clock is entirely hopeless. There are artists who can do reverse painting on glass to put in an old door panel. Other artists can paint new faces in the old manner, can do "gesso," that metallic-looking raised work found on some clock faces. And if you are interested only in the looks and do not crave a clock with named works, you can buy new works to fit your old case. If you should spot an old shelf-clock case at a sale, pick it up. It makes a fine shadow box for small articles. As for reproductions, the same thing holds here as for furniture. There are plenty around, cases made from old wood. Better take an expert with you when you go clock shopping. One more thing: Be sure your ceiling is high enough to take a full-length tall clock. Some run to eight feet.

Watches

America never excelled in turning out the beautiful watches that came over from Europe. In fact, this country did nothing about making them until about 1838, when a watch called a Pitkin watch was made in Hartford, Connecticut. It was 1853 before watches were manufactured on a large scale. However, this much can be said for American watches: they were good timekeepers and there were many cheap enough to be owned by almost anybody. The dollar watch was a typical American institution.

Up to the mid-1800s watches were imported entirely from Europe where the watch had enjoyed a long life of elegant leisure. In those early days no one relied upon his watch for the time. There was no need for split-second timing. It was a different world. If you wanted to know the time, you listened for the town crier or consulted the town clock. You might carry a small sundial in your pocket if you were outside the range of a clock. You might consult a boxlike or drum-shaped table clock with a dial on top. Later the condensed works of these small clocks were set into clumsy metal cases which could be swung from the belt, the first attempt to carry the time with you. They were called "Nuremberg eggs."

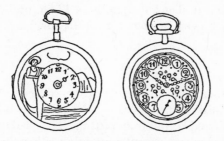

Two old watches.

The first watches were more for ornament than for real use. They were beautiful and ingenious creations of the goldsmiths, made of materials such as gold, silver, tortoise shell, enamels, crystal, shagreen (an embossed aged leather), and pinchbeck (a metal that looked like gold). They were made in various forms—shaped like crosses, hearts, skulls, or lozenge-shaped boxes. There were small watches set into earrings and rings (our ring watch is not so new), some even chimed. They were a man's declaration of position and wealth. Some fops had two watches, one for each waistcoat pocket, with elaborate fobs. Even then Switzerland excelled in watch-making although France, Germany, and England made fine watches also.

The first keyless watches were made in 1700, the first with a second hand about 1780. By 1800 the watch had become more utilitarian. Many early watches had two cases, an outer ornamental one from which the whole inner case of works and dial could be lifted. Many early American watches were silver, although I have seen an old "turnip" of the 1850s of heavily embossed plated gold. Watch chains were elaborate, with rings to hold the watch keys, for there

were still many key winders around in the 1800s. It was 1890 before
open-faced watches for both men and women came into fashion.

Women's watches changed with the styles. Perhaps many of us
can remember the chatelaine watch, the yard-long gold chain with
the slide for the watch that was tucked into the belt of the shirtwaist,
the watch that hung from its own pin on many a girlish bosom so
stylish around 1900. The radium dial did not come in until after
1896, and the wrist watch until just before World War I. While
scarcely antiques, it won't be long until collectors are after these,
too. It is safe to say that any Hamilton, Elgin, or Waltham watch
numbered under 1,000 is a buy for a collector.

Watch Papers

Here is another item of interest to the collector. Watch papers
were the small disks of paper or silk slipped in the back of a watch
case to protect it and keep it from rattling. They had other purposes,
too. One was for advertisement containing either the name of the
maker or of the repairer. The other was sentimental. A girl gave her
sweetheart or her husband a painted paper or a piece of silk for his
watch as a valentine gift or other token of affection. Sometimes
whole verses were written on watch papers. They are stilted and
flowery, but the one I like best is this from about 1730:

> Time is—the present moment well employ;
> Time was—is past—thou canst not it enjoy;
> Time future—is not and may never be;
> Time present—is the only time for thee.

Watch Holders

A gadget has just come on the market that consists of a small bell
glass with a holder on which you can hang your watch and thus
turn it into a small bedside clock. The idea is fine but not new.
There have been holders of various sorts ever since watches have
been carried. Many of them were handmade again by the women
for their men, many of them beautiful specimens of handwork,
petit point, and beads, some slipper shaped with a pocket for the

watch, some with strings to be tied around the bedpost. Such hand-made trophies were made as late as 1900. There must be many hiding in bureau drawers and old chests, bringing up the question, "What is this thing, anyway?"

Over the years watch holders and watch boxes have been found in all kinds of materials, in polished wood with a round frame for the watch, in carved wood, in cast metal with a hook for the watch and a mirror, in Dresden, in Staffordshire, in papier-mâché, silver, and even tin. They crop up unexpectedly. To collect them is at once a chase and a joy when one is found. Keep your eyes open.

A watch holder.

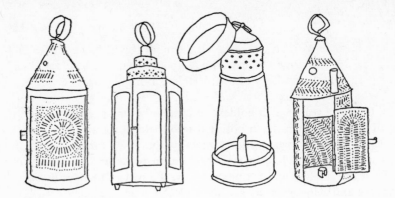

13. LAMPS AND LIGHTING

EVEN to the most primitive man light was essential after the God-given light sank below the horizon. Other means had to be developed to extend the light of the campfire, and so for centuries the burning brand sufficed. In early cultures there were lamps of oil—remember the Wise Virgins?—made from stone vessels with wicks floating in animal fat or oil. The primitive American Betty lamp was very similar to these classic lamps, a fat, grease, or oil lamp, often of brass, iron, tin, pewter, or even pottery. Sometimes it had a hinged cover and a slot for a wick which was likely to be a strip of old cloth. Betty lamps, cruises, or Phoebe lamps, which were all much alike, were made to be hung on a chair back or a hook. It is said they were also used to lower into a pot on the hearth so the housewife could see what was cooking. Betty lamps are still around in some quantity if you yearn for a bit of early American *décor*.

Earliest lighting in this country was a form of rushlight made by dipping the pith of rushes in fat. Holders for these lights had jaws for grasping the rushes and were made of iron. They are real primitives and not too easy to find.

Candlesticks have been covered in the chapters on glass, iron, brass, pewter, and silver. They were a more de-luxe lighting method and never lost their popularity even to this day. English sticks and a few early American ones were spiked to hold the candle, but most American sticks were of the socket type. Many had a push-up arrangement for the candle or a slot for poking the candle end out of the socket. Tapersticks were for small candles. Chamber sticks were the saucer-shaped ones "to light you to bed." There were hurricane candle globes then as now.

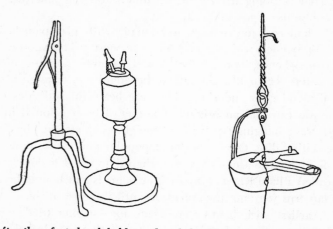

Left, a three-footed rush holder and a whale-oil lamp. *Right,* a Betty lamp.

Candles were homemade of tallow, although beeswax as well as bayberry was used. Candlemaking was a production and was often a community affair with a whole day given over to it. The candles were either hand dipped by lowering strings knotted on a rack or ring into the kettle of melted fat or wax, or they were molded by pouring the wax into tin molds through which strings had been threaded for wicks. These molds, usually of tin, are common today in multiples of two or more and are bought for various purposes, for candlesticks, electrified for sconces, or used as planters.

Candles were also used in the early candelabra and chandeliers. The latter ranged from the beautiful glass type (copied in the 1880s and nineties for gas light) with ropes and prisms possibly of Irish Waterford glass to simple ones of iron, tin, or pewter as well as the more elegant brass. One you can still pick up with a bit of looking has a center baluster of wood with tin arms for the candle sconces. Or you may find an all-tin center lighting fixture with cones of tin, plain or tooled, and flat arms for the candles. Pewter is not too common. Right now I covet an interesting chandelier in a shop I know made from a painted wooden oval ring studded with pewter cups, called a candle beam. If you are doing a room in early American I'd suggest skipping the chandelier unless you can find the right one, or else use a good reproduction.

Early lanterns, for candles, were made with glass-paned sides, bound or banded with tin or iron. The most primitive ones had horn panes—hence the name *lanthorn*. There were fine ones of iron or brass, too, rectangular in shape or hexangular or octangular with pierced metal cuffs and rings. They are beautiful additions for a hall if you can find an original. Another style of colonial indoor lantern was a hanging type with a deep glass cup attached by chains to the ceiling disk. One of the most popular and easily found lanterns is of pierced tin with a cone-shaped top and a door at the back called a Paul Revere lantern. The name is a misnomer because these lanterns were not used or made until the early 1800s.

The earliest wick lamps were made for burning whale oil or camphene, a combustible fuel made of turpentine and alcohol. They had a one- or two-pronged wick arrangement on a stubby or tall base and were used without a shade. Occasionally they had a glass bull's-eye shield for focusing the light on a book or paper. Early ones were of pewter or tin or of flint glass, free-blown three-mold. Later ones were of lacy glass or early pressed glass. They flourished from 1820 to 1860.

It was the Argand burner, however, that revolutionized the whole style of oil lighting. It was the invention of a Swiss physicist in 1784, a round burner with a round wick. The first burners were only about one inch in diameter and were used for hanging lamps, in pairs and clusters for table and mantel lamps. Many variations of the Argand burner were used as the years of lamplighting went on. It was the basis of the later Rochester lamp made in the 1880s. You'll find it in many of the kerosene lamps, the hanging lamp now so popular, the piano lamp, the student lamp, and the Gone-with-the-Wind lamp with its painted glass globe, a catchy name but a misnomer because Scarlett O'Hara never polished such a lamp at Tara. This lamp came much later.

A so-called Gone-with-the-Wind lamp.

There was another early lamp, dating from 1785, a clever little arrangement with a reservoir and burner ending in a round peg that could fit into the socket of a candlestick, thus turning it into a lamp. These peg lamps are still to be found but are not too common.

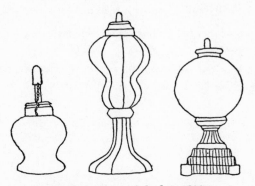

Glass lamp bases of the late 1800s.

A lamp of the 1850s with the round Argand wick was a solar lamp. It had the reservoir under the burner, the whole on top of a metal or marble column. The rim on which the round shade of the etched glass rested was hung with glass prisms.

An astral lamp of about the same period had an arm for the burner set below the reservoir. This, too, had prisms and could be quite decorative. Astral lamps, of brass, iron, china, or Sheffield plate, were the mantel lamps of the 1850s. The student lamp is a type of astral lamp. A later version was the angle lamp for kerosene.

The refining of oil seepage by a Pittsburgher in 1851 brought kerosene into the picture and started the manufacture of lamps in a big way. Many of the lamps you find today were made for kerosene or "coal oil," as it was called. The fonts are dim with it. Some still smell of it. Wicks will be either of the round type or a wide, flat wick.

Some of the Lamps You Will Find

Glass Table Lamps—Of every form and description from the small clear-glass lamp to the magnificent ones of overlay, Bohemian, Sandwich, milk, opalescent, cranberry, etc. Colored glass, of course, is the more valuable.

China Lamps—Of Dresden and other imported wares. Often combined with metal, iron and brass particularly.

Tin Lamps—Usually wall lamps with reflectors for stores and kitchens.

Pullman Lamps—From old Pullman cars—ceiling two-bracketed lamps with plain white shades.

Hall Lamps—Hanging lamps usually on chains with glass shades, round, pear-shaped, or cup-shaped. Of colored glass, swirl, hobnail, cranberry, etc.

Sparking Lamps or *Courting Lamps*—Small lamps with only a small supply of oil which would burn out in a short time and leave the lovers in the dark.

Bracket Lamp—Very popular and widely reproduced. Glass lamp fitting into a ring or cup of cast iron or brass on an arm that swings in a wall socket.

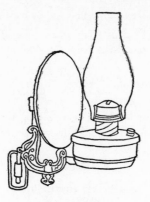

A bracket lamp.

Hanging Lamp—Popular in spite of the Victorian ornateness. Gilded metal frame and decorated shade of milk glass or other opaque glass or china. On chains. Some can be raised and lowered.

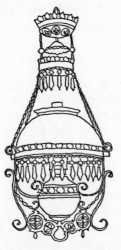

A Victorian hanging lamp.

Night Lamps or *Miniature Lamps*—Very small and very desirable.

Figure Lamp—Standard is a figure, usually brass or bronze or white metal.

Dietz Lamp—Name of prolific manufacturer of lamps, 1840 to 1860.

Petticoat Lamp—A circular lamp with a widely flaring base.

Fairy Lamp—Not an oil-burning lamp but a candle light with a domed cover resting on a saucerlike base. Of china, glass, etc. Very popular among collectors.

Bracket Gas Lights—These can be converted into fine electric side lights or door lights.

Gas Light Globes—All the lovely fluted colored glass globes are usable, also the etched-glass globes, for shades for converted oil lamps.

Lanterns

Carriage Lamps—Eagerly sought for electrifying into side lights for doorways.

Hearse Lamps—Large and fine if you can find them.

Auto Lamps—Especially the old oil and acetylene lamps for converting to side lights.

Ship's Lanterns—Both the smaller brass ones and the large red and green running lights. For outdoor use or game rooms.

Street Lamps—You can find these in various periods and styles from the old gas lights on back. I have just seen a shipment of fine old copper ones from a small English town. Beautiful!

A word about converting. In Chapter 19 I have some suggestions about this. There is nothing that cannot be done with an old lamp to make it usable. It might even be a good idea to reserve one in its original state and keep it filled with kerosene for the day when the power fails, especially if you live in the country. I do not belong to the school that advocates turning all kinds of unrelated antiques into lamps. But if you want to put the old coffee mill, the decoy duck, the toy stove, or even the china pitcher and washbasin to use, your electrician can do it for you. Be sure you call on someone who has a regard for antiques when you are having old things wired. There is a right and wrong way of doing it. I was very much impressed in examining the fixtures at Winterthur Museum, Winterthur, Delaware, by the way the electricians had done the wiring so that not a single old piece was marred or distorted in any way and the wires hidden so expertly that the illusion of candlelight was perfect.

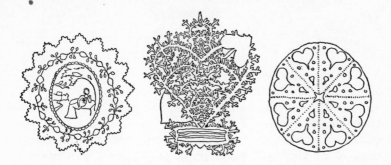

14. PICTURES, PRINTS, AND CARDS

EVERY family whose possessions have not been dissipated by many movings is almost sure to own a few old pictures of one kind or another. They may be family portraits or old framed prints that have escaped the rummage sale or perhaps lie forgotten in the attic—if there is an attic. But attics—and cellars, too—are passing from the American scene and the antique shops are the gainers. Even if one is a natural hoarder, it is a hard thing to live up to in a modern apartment or a split-level house. And so the temptation is to get rid of the junk. But before you do, take it easy. Examine what you have in those old boxes and cartons and trunks before you call in the Salvation Army or the Boy Scouts on their paper drives. Your findings may represent dollars and cents, not perhaps big figures, unless you uncover an especially rare or desirable item, but worth saving from the bonfire or the paper presses.

How are you going to know what's valuable? You won't unless you give it study. It requires much research to recognize the value in old prints and papers and such things. There are many specialists in the field. If you are willing to give the time, you may find out that what you have is more than trash. If you don't want to bother, sell it to those who do know and let them take what profit they can out of it. All I want to do in this chapter is to warn you that seemingly valueless things may fool you, and give you a hint what to look for.

Portraits

Of course family portraits you will keep, especially if they are old ones dating back before the 1900s. I don't mean the crayon enlargements made of Grandma and Grandpa in their heavy gilt frames—although the frames may be valuable. You probably have better photos of them in the family album. But older and quainter portraits of all kinds—oil, water color, pastels, wax, silhouettes, and miniatures—should be salvaged. Maybe you don't know who they were, but that doesn't matter. They still have value for you or for someone else. I have an "ancestor" whose only name I know is Charley written on the back of the frame. But he is very imposing in his Mexican War uniform over my mantel and has inspired many a good story—tongue in cheek, of course.

A silhouette.

Naturally, signed pictures bring more than unsigned ones. In colonial and federal days many portraits were the work of itinerant "limners," artists of sorts who went around the country on horseback or in wagons painting for a living, sometimes an inn sign, sometimes a portrait. It is said that they carried partly finished figures on their canvases to which they had only to add the new face. Such portraits fall into the "primitive" group done by men whose names will never be known. Names that have lived include besides the familiar Gilbert Stuart and Benjamin West William

Prior of Maine, Isaac Wetherby who "went West" in 1840, Lorenzo Somerby, Jonathan Wheeler, and Ruth Henshaw Bascom of Massachusetts, Joseph Davis of New Hampshire, and Joseph Stock to name only a few. It is not likely that you'll turn up one of their pictures—but you never know.

There may be a forgotten miniature done on ivory, bone, porcelain, or plain cardboard, perhaps crude and unsigned, hiding in an old bureau. Treasure it. Or you may find a water-color portrait done in profile, usually the work of an amateur. Young ladies were schooled in this work. They were also taught wax work, and a portrait in bas-relief wax will be a real find. Then there were the silhouettes, a vogue from 1775 to 1845, cheap substitutes for oil portraits. The French were skilled silhouettists and in America there were many who could do silhouettes freehand, although there was a machine that did them with the use of a reducing lens. There were itinerant silhouettists, too, such as the New Englander Moses Chapman. The story is told of a woman with no hands who covered the eastern seaboard making her living making silhouettes which she cut with her toes. The results of her labors are now quite valuable. Silhouettes were either cut from black and mounted on white, or white cutouts mounted on black. Often the figure was filled with a water-color background. Collectors go for silhouettes in a big way, especially if they have some unusual feature to recommend them. Some look for signed names of Edouart, Peale's Museum, Bache, Day, or Brown.

Daguerreotypes—or tintypes—the invention of a French photographer, L. J. M. Daguerre, in 1839 put silhouettes out of business. They are only three or four generations old. Unfortunately the likeness fades. That is why you see so many old empty daguerreotype cases around. You wonder why they have been kept. But they are becoming collectors' items because some of them were quite beautifully made and embellished of a pressed composition material. If you have any with pictures you treasure, keep them out of the light. These first photos were good likenesses but stiffly posed, and often with much added in the way of adornment and background. I have one of my mother aged three, and once in confidence she told me that the string of gold beads around her neck had been added by the photographer. She'd never owned a necklace at that age. Any worse than the "retouching" that modern photographers do?

Other Paintings

Don't discard any oils or water colors, landscapes, religious subjects, ships, or still lifes done before 1875, no matter how crude they may look to you. These are the "folk art," the primitives, which are being eagerly collected now. You may find them painted on wood, tin, sacking, silk, or velvet, or even embroidered. You may find an old "mourning" picture of a weeping figure beside a weeping willow and a tombstone inscribed to the memory of a dead-and-gone loved one. These pictures were often what is called "seminary art," done by the young ladies who learned to paint as a part of their "finishing" process.

It isn't likely you'll find an old sign kicking around, but if you do, don't burn it up for firewood. And if you should happen to have a cigar-store Indian or other figure tucked away in a far corner, bring him out. These wooden figures have jumped to the three-figure class. Even a run-of-the-mill one will bring $500. They are rare and they are wanted.

Scrimshaw was another medium for the amateur artist. This was scratch drawing on whalebone done by the sailors on their long voyages. It is found to a great extent on busks, those stiff slats worn by women in lieu of a corset to flatten their stomachs. Any bit of scrimshaw has a ready market.

Fractur

Fractur, from the German word used for an old type face, includes the illuminated papers and books of the Pennsylvania Dutch who brought over with them from Germany and Switzerland the art that flourished in the monasteries. By the time it became a more or less commercial thing with the certificates of birth and baptism and marriage printed on paper to be filled in by the individual, little of the original beauty of the work was left. But there are still to be found old hand-drawn and hand-colored Taufscheins, Geburtscheins, Trauscheins, Vorschrifts, Haus-segens (house blessings), mottoes, songbooks, merit awards, etc. They are typical Pennsylvania folk art with hearts, tulips, birds, and angels in happy company. Collectors will grab up anything you have in this line.

A Fractur birth certificate.

The Shakers had a similar picture art which they displayed in their "spirit drawings" with symbols of doves, harps, trumpets, wings, etc., to interpret a religious message. Ohio, Maine, and New York should produce these.

In the Far West there was a primitive art inspired by the Spanish. You'll find in New Mexico and other western states the same things you find in Mexico, holy pictures, *santos,* images of the saints painted on tin or wood as well as canvas. As many were done by amateur *santeros,* they have the crude appeal that the preservers of primitive American art are looking for.

Prints
Currier and Ives

I doubt if there is a family who has made a home in America for sixty years or more who has not had a Currier and Ives print hanging on its walls. It was the cheap and popular home decoration of the country from 1835 to 1907. Its fame rests on the fact that Currier and Ives was the first large-scale producer of lithographs, a cheap substitute for engraving. These prints were printed from a special porous stone imported from Bavaria, the picture delineated upon it with crayons that resisted the acid and water bath used to wash away the background and leave the picture in relief.

Before lithography, pictures were made from engraved copper plates or printed from wood blocks. All old prints have value and many have tremendous value. It is too big a subject to go into here, but if you are interested, read the books on the subject. You'll learn about mezzotints, stipple, aquatints, etchings, and color prints. You'll read about Bartolozzi and Baxton, who made the color prints and such things as the famous "Cries of London" by Wheatley. It is a fascinating subject, and a visit to a printshop for general browsing will do you no harm. However, what I want to discuss here are the more available types of prints likely to have been passed down in the average American home or picked up in the village antique shop. So, back to Currier and Ives.

Nathaniel Currier, born in 1813, and apprenticed to a print maker in Boston, left to open a shop with a partner named Stodart in 1834, but a year later went into business for himself in New York. Until 1857 all prints were signed N. Currier, but in that year he took on as partner James Ives, related to him by marriage, and Currier and Ives flourished under that name, carried on by the sons of both men until 1907. During this period the firm put out thousands of subjects and hundreds of thousands of prints. One subject alone, "Darktown Capers," sold 75,000 prints. It is said they turned out three new subjects a week and to date 7,000 of these subjects have been found. They include:

Portraits—Of famous people and the presidents. A portrait of Dr. Wm. **P.** Dewey of the University of Pennsylvania is supposed to be the first print issued by the firm of N. Currier (1834) and is rare and valuable. Presidents up to Lincoln are worth more than the later ones.

Horses and Horse Racing—Also fox hunting. The print, "Peytona and Fashion," showing the famous race of 1845 in good condition and large size might bring in over $2,000.

Transportation—Clipper ships, steamboats, trains, Hudson and Mississippi River steamboats are all valuable.

Sports—Prize fighting, baseball, skating, boat races, fishing, hunting, etc. "Life of a Hunter—A Tight Fix," one of the most valuable of all the prints.

Fires—Conflagrations, fire engines, and fire fighting. "Burning of the New York Crystal Palace," is a good one.

Nature—American scenes. Farm scenes. Seasons. Winter pictures bring more.

Sentimental—Lovers, family scenes, married life. Plenty of these around. In the lower brackets.

Children—Hundreds of "Little" pictures, "Little Flora," "Little Beggar," and so on. Cheapest of all.

Fruits and Flowers—Not in too much demand, but not too common.

Animals—Not too hard to find.

Political and Cartoons—All kinds and available.

Religious and Moralistic—Holy pictures and the Intemperance series, one of the most famous being "The Drunkard's Progress."

There are plenty of Currier and Ives prints to be bought for $5, but a few will bring into the thousands. It would pay to study what you have and compare it with a good price list. Be sure you are not being fooled with a reproduction. Read the fine print.

How did this firm manage to produce in such quantity? They had on call a staff of proficient artists among whom Fanny Palmer is a name most remembered. Occasionally an artist of more than average ability lent his talent to the firm, such as the painter of a print called "The Husking," which comes nearer to a well-executed oil painting of the period.

Prints came off the press in black and white and were colored by hand. The production line consisted mostly of women, each one adding a color to the print as it passed under her hand. Some of the work was farmed out to needy artists, who tinted the small size for one cent a piece. Prints, but not every subject, were made in three sizes, large folio 18 x 27, medium 13 x 20, and small 7.8 x 12.8. Prices vary according to sizes. The finished prints were sold everywhere, even peddled from door to door in pushcarts. They found their way to England, France, and Germany. They were indeed the "people's choice" in art for that period.

Other Prints

Contemporary with Currier and Ives were other print makers, Kellogg, Sarony and Major, Haskell and Allen, Duval and Prang, all of whom brought out prints similar to Currier and Ives but not nearly so numerous or worth so much today.

The original Audubon prints were, of course, engravings and worth their weight in gold if you could find them today. But a series of his birds in colored lithographs came out in 1839 as well as his "Quadrupeds of America," in 1844. Worth saving and keeping an eye out for. There were other bird prints by Alex Wilson in 1808–1814 and the Gould bird prints are well known.

Fashion prints from *Godey's Lady's Book, Peterson's,* and *Leslie's* magazines of the mid-1800s have flooded the market but are still worth saving.

Fruit and flower prints were supplied from the old nurserymen's catalogues, such as Landreth's in 1832, Mrs. E. M. Wirt's "Flora's Dictionary" of 1837, and D. M. Dewey's list of almost 150 prints of fruit, berries, and flowers supplied to various seedmen for their catalogues.

These prints are only a few of the most popular and most likely to be found, but there were many others. If in doubt, take them to your library or museum for identification or to a reputable print shop.

Maps

Any old map is valuable to somebody. Of special interest are the local maps of a region, the county and township maps. In my own county in Pennsylvania a volume of township maps printed in 1874 has the names and boundaries of the property owners on each township map and a list of the businessmen is printed on the margin. A book I paid $10 for a few years ago is now worth $30. Dealers are buying up such books and selling the pages for $5 to $10 apiece. This is only one example of what can be done with old maps. Maybe your historical society would be happy to get any you might find.

Greeting Cards

The first greeting cards in this country were valentines. Christmas cards did not appear until about 1867, although they had been used in England as early as 1846. One of the big names to remember is Louis Prang, who came over here from England about the time Raphael Tuck and Sons and Marcus Ward were putting out English cards. These three names are big ones in Christmas-card history. It was Marcus Ward for whom the artist Kate Greenaway worked. Her quaint little bonneted and long-skirted children have become famous in many ways. Her work is to be found on both Christmas cards and valentines, as is the work of her fellow artist Walter Crane.

Curiously enough old Christmas cards were not always Christmasy. Santa Claus looked like a somber old monk on many of them. Any pretty scene seemed to answer the purpose, as did flowers, birds, even Japanese figures, anything "pretty" to carry the Christmas message. In fact, some designs were used indiscriminately for both Christmas cards and valentines.

A Kate Greenaway Christmas card.

The origin of the valentine goes back to early Christian times and was based on a pagan feast called the Lupercalia, which the church adopted for February 14, the day of the martyrdom of Bishop Valentine in A.D. 270. Love messages crop up all through the Middle Ages celebrating that day. In this country the first written valentine was recorded in 1684. But the real history of American valentines does not begin until the mid-1700s. They were mostly homemade, painted, pinpricked, of cutwork, or folded ingeniously to make rebuses. The greetings were flowery, most often in verse, and they were delivered by hand. The Pennsylvania Dutch were adept in this lacy cutwork, and some very fine valentines are still to be found framed and hanging in Pennsylvania parlors.

Lithographed valentines came in about 1840 with names like T. W. Strong, Turner, and Fisher, and Elton and Co. Room was usually left on these printed valentines for the sender to write his own message. It is to an energetic college girl turned career woman of the 1840s, Esther Howland of Worcester, Massachusetts, that we owe the vogue of the lace-paper valentine which set the style for years. Her story is worth a book in itself. Inspired by a fancy English valentine she had received, she set to work to make her own. Soon she had a small plant going in her own home with girls working on a production line to paste up the hearts and doves, etc., on the beautiful embossed "blanks" which she imported from England and Germany. At one time she was doing $100,000 worth of business a year. Her valentines were always in good taste. They set a style. Many of them had a letter H on them in some hidden spot as a trademark, and later the initials N. E. V. Co. She also made birthday cards, Christmas cards, New Year's cards, and booklets of all sorts. She could be called the mother of the greeting-card business.

Comic valentines go back quite early, when they were called caricatures. Strangely enough they are not too different from the cheap comic valentines of today with the same caustic and insulting verses upon them. It is interesting that English comics were not popular in America. English humor did not strike our funny bones.

From 1860 on the valentine followed the Victorian trend of fussiness with elaborate cards, boxes, fans, and paper ones that worked. If you are going to collect valentines, you may play the field and discover far more than I have described here. But I hope what I have written will open up the subject and save some old-fashioned love token from being burned up or sold to the paper collector.

Other Paper Items

To be on the safe side I would say just this, never throw out any accumulations of old papers. Here are things to salvage:

Scrapbooks	Theater programs
Catalogues	Invitations to Public Affairs
Trade Cards	Old Stamped or Franked Envelopes
Old Magazines	Account Books
Old Newspapers	Drawing Books
Playing Cards and Games	Autographs
Political Fliers	Civil War Data
Documents	Labels
Posters	Circus Handbills
	Old Music and Song Books

Some may be worth nothing, but people are advertising all the time for data of this sort, and it might pay to sort out what you have and watch the ads in the magazines. If you have enough, it might pay to advertise them yourself.

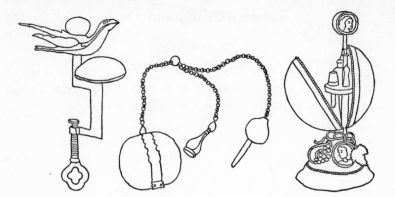

15. HANDWORK

FROM all accounts the ladies of America have always been busy bees either because of necessity and the rigors of pioneer days or because to keep one's fingers busy with some kind of handwork was the proper thing for every lady to do. Many of the projects taken up by the women in colonial, federal, and even Victorian times were born of necessity, but many more were sheer expressions of artistic (?) yearnings.

Needlework has, of course, always been a womanly skill. To be a fine seamstress, "to sit on a cushion and sew a fine seam," was every girl's ambition. She started young. A well-educated girl was supposed to have a repertoire of fine stitches at her command. She was first shown how to turn a seam and finish it, then how to draw threads and hemstitch, to gather and sew on gathers, to do herringbone stitch, to make buttonholes, to sew on buttons, to darn, to tuck, to whip, and to sew on a frill. Many of these things she learned early on her sampler, doing the rows of "sample" stitching in colored wools or silks on canvas or linen or a sort of gauze sold for the purpose. These were called "exemplars" in the old days.

In England, samplers were long and narrow, and until the weaving looms grew wider they were the same in America. But for the most part what we find today are square. One of the earliest samplers has been preserved at Plymouth. It was made by Lorea Standish, a

Pilgrim daughter, and it has a quaint little embroidered verse upon it as did many of the early ones.

Besides the lines of stitches which were executed in tent stitch, cross-stitch, satin stitch, and outline, whole alphabets and figures in several kinds of lettering were embroidered. Such samplers were popular in the early 1700s. Combined with the name, date, letters, numbers, and so on, the sampler might display human figures, trees, fruits, curious flowers and vines, birds, animals, and even houses, especially schoolhouses. This was the place for the righteous motto.

Left, a lace sampler. *Right,* a needlework sampler.

There are many samplers in existence because they were made well into the 1800s. Some are more interesting than others, but a family piece is of course of greatest importance. You are lucky if you own one. Many old samplers show the signs of age, moths have eaten the wools, sun has faded the colors. But they are still worth saving and putting behind glass. Perhaps you will find a sampler with insets of homemade lace or even an unfinished one where the patience of the young seamstress gave out. Even these should be cherished.

Of something of the same character as the sampler is the door panel, or door towel, *handtuchen* the Pennsylvania Dutch call it, for these embroidered show towels are numerous in the Dutch country, though they are also found in New York, New England, and Ohio. They were a fancy long, narrow towel to be "shown," not used, and contrary to the opinion of many Pennsylvania Dutch fanciers they were not of German origin. They are closer to the Scandinavian or to the Swiss in their peasant designs, which were embroidered in white, red or blue. Wooden boxes to hold such towels are common in Switzerland. In Pennsylvania, they were often used as a cover for the family roller towel.

Other stitches used by our early seamstresses were stump work, a padded, raised pattern work; crewelwork, which was embroidery done with fine wools on homespun and used extensively for bed hangings, coverlets, chair cushions, hangings, and purses; flame stitch, a sort of zigzag stitch in colored threads which entirely covered the fabric; tent stitch, a short, slanting stitch worked from left to right; turkey work, a tufted stitch to imitate the "Turkey carpets"; and quilting. This last was a great favorite, as it gave thickness and weight to fine fabrics. Women's petticoats, apron panels for dresses, men's vests, coverlets, and many other things were quilted so beautifully that plain materials were turned into fabrics that resembled brocades. Later, from 1800 on, quilting was widely used for all our patchwork and appliquéd quilts.

Candlewicking was another form of needlework, the tufts either cut or left looped. But of all the fancywork indulged in by ladies from 1675 to 1835 petit point was the favorite. Most women kept something on their frames for leisure hours, an embroidered picture perhaps of Washington or Franklin, a seat for a chair, a top for a stool, a panel for a pole screen for the fireplace. One subject called "the fishing lady" was a favorite for these panels. Embroidered pictures in petit point and other stitches were very much the thing in the early 1800s. They were done with silks, chenille, and crewels on satin with perhaps some tinsel threads mixed in and were often memorial pieces with tombs and weeping willows and disconsolate figures. Other embroidered pictures showed flowers, ships, biblical scenes, maps, or sentimental subjects. They were a test of a young lady's skill and education. For the most part they were self-designed and are as primitive as many of the oils and water colors. Later, patterns were sold for them with the faces painted in.

Women have always knitted. In the early days they had first to spin what they were going to knit with. While the old spinning and wool wheels still ornament our parlors, their days of use are over.

It was quite a process from the shearing of the wool or the drying of the flax to the finished thread or yarn. We wonder how those early housewives got time after knitting all the family hose and gloves and scarves to express themselves in anything beautiful, but they did. Two pieces left over from home knitting days which are of antique interest are the niddy noddy, a short wooden rod with a crosspiece at each end set at right angles, and the swift, a contrivance with two revolving wheels in a frame. Both were for winding wool.

Lace was made in this country but not to the extent that it was in Europe. Some early forms of pillow lace are to be found, but what you will come upon in more abundance is the lace darned on net which was used for fichus, caps, veils, and baby caps. Later on, by 1840, the French crocheted filet lace was made, and later yet the Irish crochet. Embroideries of cutwork or Honiton guipure gave a lacy appearance to tablecloths or towel borders. Appliqué came in about 1850 and there was a Victorian furore for *broderie anglaise,* a white embroidery on white. Tatting from a small bobbin was made by the mile for edgings. Many of these types of handwork have survived to the present day and are familiar.

One skill which has almost died out is netting. This is the knotted work done on the same principle as the fishermen's nets or the southern hammock. It was used particularly for those graceful tasseled canopies for the tester and field beds, for counterpane ruffles, and in a smaller way for mitts, hair snoods, and fly nets for horses. It is not a difficult thing to master, but it requires a set of instruments, a steel needle, and a mesh stick of bone, wood, or ivory. Such sets were kept and carried in a special bag or case. If you should happen upon such a set now, you'll know what it is. They are hard to find. I happen to know a New England woman who inherited this skill from her grandmother and she tells me she would be lost if anything happened to her tools.

Beadwork was another accomplishment of the ladies from colonial days on. Bead bags and purses were as beautiful as paintings, so were pincushion tops, chair seats, slipper toes, and watch holders for hanging beside the bed. Did your grandmother make misers' purses knit from silk with steel or iridescent beads? They were in two parts and were divided from each other by sliding metal rings. I am sure there must be some of these around today.

From 1860 to 1890 a form of cross-stitch on canvas called Berlin work became a craze. It was used to make many things, such as bags, chair seats, cushions, stool tops, lambrequins, men's slippers, waistcoats, and even rugs. Patterns were sold for it. Later perforated cardboard patterns came out through which the wool was stitched. These were the mottoes like "Home Sweet Home, God Bless Our Home," etc., usually framed in walnut with carving and crisscrossed corners. Cardboard patterns were also sold for bookmarks.

Quilts and Coverlets

Here are antiques you will find in abundance. American coverlets go back to pioneer days when they were the chief warm covers for the beds. Because they were made of sturdy stuff, some early ones have survived, but the finest have found their way into private collections and museums. You will find, however, many dating from the 1800s. The South was particularly active in this hand-weaving

Three well-known quilt patterns.

art. Back in the Appalachian hills the pioneer women set up their looms, and the patterns they used have been passed down from generation to generation like fine family silver. They have fascinating names, Double Muscadine, Muscadine Hulls, Wheel of Fortune, Ocean Wave, Sunrise, Lover's Knot, and Frenchman's Fancy, to name only a few. The cardboard patterns, or "drafts," as

they were called, are now yellow with age. Punched with hiero-
glyphics for the weaver, they remind one of a choreographer's score.

Coverlets were woven at home in the northern colonies, too, but
you are more likely to find the output of the professional weaver of
the 1830s and 1840s when you go hunting. In those years the weaver
was a journeyman or itinerant who went from town to town setting
up his loom and taking orders from the housewives who brought
him their own linen thread and homespun, home-dyed woolen
yarns. The linen was used for the warp, and it is recorded that a
double-woven spread might take forty pounds of linen thread set up
in 2,000 threads on the loom. A good weaver could turn out one or
more coverlets a week. Wools were home-dyed with vegetable dyes
made from the products of the fields and gardens, madder for red,
wild indigo for blue, osage orange for yellow, walnut bark for
brown, and many other plants.

Coverlets were made double not only for warmth but so that they
could be reversed. When the jacquard loom came in, a single coverlet could be turned wrong side out and show the design in reverse.
Because the first looms were not wide you'll find many old coverlets
pieced down the middle. It was the custom to weave the name of
the maker or owner or both, also the date, and place into the border
or one corner of the cover. Such signed coverlets are desirable because they establish authenticity without a doubt.

Patterns run from severe blocks and plaids to elaborate floral
motifs, paisley-like scrolls, birds, mottoes, farmhouses, and even state
houses along the border. One of the finest of coverlets is the *E Pluri-
bus Unum* design with eagles.

Sometimes you may find only half a coverlet or one in bad condition in spots. Don't spurn them. Even a remnant of an old cover
is worth saving. I have seen pieces of coverlets used with plain
material to make bed coverings, to upholster an old rocker, or made
into cushion tops.

Just when patched or pieced quilts came into general use in this
country is not definitely established, but mention of them goes back
to the early 1700s. "Coverlids" and silk quilts were things of value
mentioned in wills and inventories. But the best quilts we are most
likely to own or to find are those of the 1800s, especially from 1830
to 1850.

The Middle West seemed to excel in quilt making. In those thrifty days, when everything had to be put to use, women saved their pieces from their home dressmaking for their "crazy" pieced quilts, which were usually an economic chore rather than an artistic pastime. It was the patterned patched or appliquéd quilts that were outlets for artistic expression. Often they bought new material for such quilts, choosing sturdy, color-fast cottons. For backing they would use a gay-patterned percale or calico.

The quilt was usually pieced or patched at home in odd moments, but when the top was finished the quilting was apt to be a communal or neighborly affair. Top, backing, and filling were basted together and fastened to a large frame with rollers around which as many as a dozen women could sit. Tongues and fingers flew together. A famous old wood-block print, called "A Quilting in West Virginia," shows such a party with the women busy and men and children at play around them. There is a record of a ten-day quilting party in Narragansett in 1792.

Names of the old quilt patterns are as fascinating as the coverlet names but there are more of them. Hundreds have been recorded.

One corner of a woven coverlet with the names of the maker and owner woven in.

The rose was a favorite subject, and in a listing we find twenty rose names, such as Rose of Sharon, Dixie Rose, Mexican Rose, Rose of Le Moine. In the same list are forty star patterns. Mentioned also are sentimental things such as Lover's Knot, Wedding Ring, Friendship Ring, and Lover's Rose. We have perhaps heard of such patterns as Log Cabin, Windmill, Fox and Geese, Irish Chain, Star of Bethlehem, Princess Feather, Jacob's Ladder, and Jacob's Coat, but have you ever come across a Puss-in-the-Corner, The Drunkard's Path, Ticktacktoe, or Tangled Garters? They all meant something to the women who patched or quilted them, but one would need to be an expert to recognize them though many have been documented.

In a recent exhibition of old quilts I was interested in seeing how many of them were signed and dated in ink. One unusual quilt was patched in 1845 for a wedding gift from sister to sister. In the large center square are the names of the couple and the story of their romance written in verse. There are other flowery verses in each corner square. It was a very happy quilt with the pattern of roses appliquéd from a rose-sprigged calico.

There were friendship quilts and autograph quilts with names of famous people inked upon the patches. Apparently even then the VIPs were bothered by autograph hunters.

Quilting was often done "by eye," but many women relied upon pattern blocks which were blacked and pressed lightly upon the quilt top. You may come across some of these old blocks or the patchwork patterns and stencils cut in tin or cardboard. You can find quilting frames, too, if you yearn for them. Quilting, while not a popular craft, is still done. Many church groups will quilt your coverlet for you to raise money. So if you are lucky enough to find a pieced top ready to be quilted or even a box of cut patches, you can have yourself an old quilt that has never been used.

Rugs

The first American floor coverings were painted floor cloths which were not unlike our modern oilcloth. Rag carpets did not come into use until 1776, but they were used for more than one hundred years. If your memory is as long as mine, you may remember the carpet balls of rags all torn and sewn together waiting to be sent to the mill to be woven with a strong linen or cotton warp into carpet runners which could be sewn into room-size carpets. But in the early days they were woven at home.

Early rugs were of three kinds. The first was a heavy cloth backing on which other material was stitched to make it thick and warm. There were "button" rugs with small rag disks sewn one above another, "tongue" rugs with overlapping tongue-shaped pieces, shaggy or fluff rugs. The second type was made by interlacing strips of rags by braiding, crocheting, or knitting. The third was the familiar hooked rug, where material was pulled through the mesh of a loosely woven material and left in cut or uncut loops. All of these rugs used up old material in their making and were a thrifty answer to household ornamentation.

Braided rugs, which went faster, used up a lot of leftover clothes in the course of a year. The women dyed old underwear to get their effects. There were many variations and tricks for such rugs, which could be round, oval, or square. Because a well-braided rug made from strong materials had many years of use in it—I still have one made by my own grandmother for a birthday forty years ago and in almost constant though careful use—they can be found at many a country sale. Of course there are new ones and women who will make them for you if you bring them the rags.

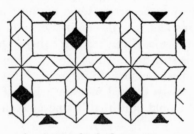

A primitive hooked-rug pattern.

In the Blue Ridge Mountains they made a rug called a tufted rug with work like candlewicking. Patterns were outlined with tufts cut or uncut and backgrounds filled in with them.

Although a carpet factory was started in Philadelphia as early as 1791 and carpetmaking was encouraged, the American housewife continued to make her own floor coverings for many years. In the homes where there was leisure for the lady of the house, women embroidered rugs, using wools in cross-stitch on backings of heavy material. Two of the most famous of these rugs are the Pliny rug made in Champlain which took four years (1808 to 1812) to make, and the Caswell rug, now in the Metropolitan Museum in New York City. This rug was made by a Vermont woman named Zeruah Guernsey in 1835. She later became Mrs. Caswell. The rug has 76 eighteen-inch squares each with a different pattern, and is a masterpiece of color and design.

There are antique Indian rugs, too, the early ones woven by the Navajos from native wool and patterned with the ravelings of red woolen garments brought over by the Spanish. Modern Indian rugs are similar, but the mellow coloring of the old ones with their pinks, green-blues, sage green, beige, and honey colors cannot be equaled.

Few hooked rugs found today will date much before 1850, although they, too, were made in colonial days. The number was probably limited, because such a rug took a lot of doing. They first had to find a basic material to be hooked. If they used linen, they had to spin the thread and weave the cloth. Sometimes they used sacking. Then they had to dye their materials to get a variety of colors. Then the material had to be cut into strips, and then they had to have a hook made for the looping. It was usually a homemade affair of bone or wood or perhaps a porcupine quill. Sometimes an old nail was forged into a hook. I've seen such a one just as good today as when it was made, even better than the ones you can buy now.

As for designs, the hooker made her own, and, what is more, she made them up as she went along, which accounts for the lopsided look of many antique rugs as well as for the afterthoughts in the design. This is what makes them primitive.

New England, Nova Scotia, and the provinces of eastern Canada, the mid-Atlantic states, and the southern mountain regions were the great rug-making areas. Patterns were influenced by the people of these districts. Thus from Quebec you got a French feeling in the floral designs, in the mid-Atlantic states it was Dutch, in Virginia English, to the Far South Spanish, and in the Far West Indian. A housewife drew what she saw—the posies in her garden, the cat or dog on the mat, the barnyard animals and birds, and perhaps a patriotic emblem. Many marine motifs were used on rugs, and this is explained by the fact that sailors on their long voyages took to hooking as a pastime.

Rugs were oblong, oval, round, or square. There was a semi-circular door rug often with the word "Welcome" on it. There were geometric rugs aimed probably at using up odds and ends of rags in a hurry.

The heyday of the hooked rug came in twenty years after the Civil War. It was during this period that a man named Edward Frost went through New England selling hooked-rug patterns stamped on burlap. It is said that he had several hundred designs which were bought up and are being used today. An original "Frost" rug means something to a collector. He was followed by a man named Pond from Biddeford, Maine, and in 1885 the Ross Rug Company of Dayton, Ohio, went into manufacturing rug patterns. The making of hooked rugs has taken a new spurt in the last twenty years, and some of the new ones are quite as nice as—if not nicer than —the antique ones. The market for the old ones has been pretty well combed. Collectors consider a rug made from 1775 to 1825 as antique, from 1825 to 1875 as early, and 1875 to 1900 as late. Anything made from then on is "modern."

If you are buying an old rug, be sure it is not going to fall to pieces before you get it on the floor. Most old rugs are badly worn, but unless the backing is brittle with age the holes and ravelings can be mended—if the rug is worth it. Colors will probably be faded but they will perk up with a good dry cleaning. Some people hesitate to walk on these old rugs and they hang them on the wall. I will go along only partly with this practice, although it is a fact that many hooked wall pictures were made to be looked at and not to be walked on.

Sewing Accessories

Many interesting antiques have come out of the sewing basket. Take pincushions alone. I never realized how diverse and fascinating they could be until I went through a collection recently. It covered years from a medieval petit-point cushion to a patchwork tomato, from pillow cushions to chatelaines. Pillow cushions were often beaded, some were cross-stitched or embroidered in silks. They were square, round, heart-shaped, shield-shaped, or star-shaped. They were divided into sections like the petals of a flower. They were shaped like animals. You can imagine the ladies who made them cudgeling their brains to think of something different for that pin-cushion gift.

Hanging pincushions were often simple balls of stuffing covered with a knitted or crocheted cover with date and initials worked into the stitches. They were hung by a knitted cord or ribbon on a chair arm, a bureau knob, or a belt. The finest of the hanging cushions were the chatelaines with a specially designed ring to hold the ball cushion and to which was attached a chain and a clasp to be fitted over the belt. These were mostly of silver, and again names and initials were engraved upon them. Some of the chatelaines which have outlasted the cushions are still to be found.

Of course any dated cushion is worth far more than an undated one. If the data were not incorporated in the stitching they were often filled in by the pins. Cushions with the pins still in them tell the tale, or perhaps only the rusty marks of the pins are left.

Since the pincushion is almost a thing of the past, even the small bran-filled ones sold not too many years ago are worth saving.

There are collectors of thimbles, and any unusual one, such as a topless one, a china one, or one belonging to a well-known person, is a collectors' item. The same goes for scissors. An interesting item to trace down is the name scissors, made from 1825 to 1835, with a girl's name wrought in the handle. Darning eggs can be fascinating, too. Sewing birds are popular and available but growing costly. Needlecases, like the pincushions, were apt to be homemade affairs, made to fold or roll up into compact little cases with covers of leather, felt, silk, or embroidered linen with inner leaves of pinked flannel to hold the needles. They were called "housewives." I once picked up a darling little needlecase in Mexico, of all places, of red-and-white bone, shaped like a furled umbrella with a screw-off handle. There is another type of workcase called by the French of the nineteenth century a *nécessaire,* a small box just large enough to hold thimble, bodkin, needles, scissors, etc. I have seen a beauty, probably of French origin, in the shape of an enameled egg set on an onyx and ormolu base and opening to disclose a compact setup of sewing necessities on a central standard. I have also in my own possession an amusing leather box about the size of a cigarette pack gilt-embossed and titled "The Lady's Companion," which I picked off a dusty shelf for fifty cents. So you see small sewing things are around if you look closely for them.

Sewing baskets, bags, and boxes are legion. I find such things fun to look for because they are novel and not usually expensive. Again I mention a box of my own, of round cardboard covered with Chinese paper and with spikes of common nails inside to hold the spools of thread. I bought it for a quarter but I wouldn't part with it for many dollars. In the *Godey's Lady's Book* period and earlier ladies wore fancy sewing aprons with vertical slits in front for a deep pocket which virtually made them into sewing bags. They probably wore out before they were retired, but an old trunk might be hiding one.

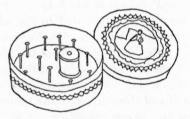

A Victorian spool box.

Another sewing accessory is the spool cabinet, the kind with the tier of shallow drawers from which the stores dispensed the cotton and sewing silk. These have become very popular. Usually the name of the maker is on them, but it can be removed with the old varnish or painted over. Such sets of shallow drawers are useful for many things—photographs, papers, maps, mats, stationery, or even for sewing things.

And while we are on the topic of sewing, don't neglect any old materials you happen to come upon. Occasionally at sales you will be offered some pieces of handwoven linen, old checked tablecloths washed to a mellowed red or blue with fringed napkins to match, or even unused dress materials. Not long ago I got a fine black silk suit out of a partly made dress of heavy black grosgrain with some of the unused material rolled on a cardboard tube—all for $7. Old silks were not "weighted" and do not crack over the years. You are not likely to find any copper-printed chintzes lying around—although you never know. If so, you have a real find. But there may be lengths of those delightful little printed calicoes and percales used to line quilts. Country stores will often come up with a bolt or two. Grab them. These patterns are being reproduced today but nothing quite equals the quaintness of the old ones.

Other Handwork

The ladies of the nineteenth century were busy with many other things besides the needle. I shall list some of their activities briefly just as signposts of what to look for and recognize in the attic or to pick up at a country sale.

Artificial Flowers—Made from silk and velvet cuttings and framed in a shadow box.

Papyrotamia—Paper cutwork, often quite fine.

Stenciling—In bronze and gold and colored oils on trays, furniture, etc. Worth a volume in itself.

Painting on Velvet—For framed pictures, lambrequins, etc.

Featherwork—Pictures made from available feathers of barnyard fowls and birds.

Shellwork—Decorated picture frames, boxes, etc.

Waxwork—Often whole pictures were done in wax in half-relief, but more often flowers and fruit were molded and encased in a glass dome to give elegance to a Victorian parlor.

India Painting—Cutout prints pasted on boxes, etc., to be combined with other decoration.

Découpage—Another form of cutout work where trays, boxes, whole pieces of furniture were covered with colored pictures cut from prints and books, etc. More of a French art, but followed here to some extent.

Transfer Work—A sort of decalcomania process done by soaking colored chromolithographs or steel engravings in water, then pressing them on a tacky surface until the printed picture comes off. Often done on glass for clock faces, pictures, etc.

Pressed Flowers—Used in shadow boxes or lamp screens.

Transparencies—Pressed flowers, grasses, or ferns put between two pieces of plain or frosted glass, to be hung in a window. Sometimes glass was painted in a design or transparent picture.

Spatterwork—Inks or dyes were spattered by flicking them from a comb for background around a pattern cut out for the purpose.

Fretwork—A man's hobby, done with a fretsaw to make ornate cutout shelves, brackets, picture frames, etc., from soft woods.

Quillwork—Done with rolled bits of paper plus wax or some other substance to form a picture.

A quillwork sconce.

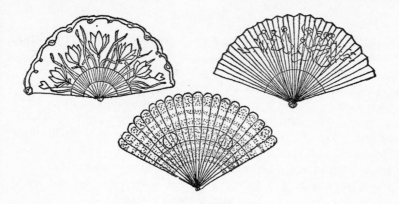

16. FADS AND FRIPPERIES

I N THIS chapter I want to list a lot of delightful bits of old-time finery, some valuable, some not so valuable, but all interesting from the point of view of the antique lover.

Jewelry

Aside from the valuable pieces of gem-set jewelry which have been handed down in most families with respect, there are usually other pieces, probably all nineteenth century, discarded because broken or considered too old-fashioned. I am all for getting out these old pieces and restoring them if possible, for there is no time when a handsome old piece of jewelry cannot be worn with pride.

Very little Georgian—that is pre-1800—jewelry is available. What you'll find is mostly Victorian, and later pieces from 1890 to the early 1900s which are acquiring age and interest from collectors. Victorian jewelry runs the gamut of elaborate, showy pieces of the early days of Victoria's reign to the mourning jewelry that marked the death of the Prince Consort. The middle years are the best.

Here in America what we did not import from England were copies of the Victorian styles. The gold rush in 1849 made gold a favorite adornment and gave the American jewelry business a big

boost. The big manufacturing centers were New York, Providence,
Rhode Island, and Philadelphia.

So let's see what a visit to a dealer who specializes in old jewelry
might bring forth. You'll find cameos, the familiar kind cut from
shell as well as some from lava and intaglio cuttings on many kinds
of stones. The large cameo brooches were often miniature master-
pieces. But simpler cameos were used for rings, earrings, chain slides,
etc. You'll find coral, lots of it, pale pink to deep red. You'll find
jet—a form of vegetable matter akin to coal—for which black glass
was often substituted. So be careful. It is said you can test jet in
water—it sinks slowly. You might possibly find a piece of bog oak
from Ireland and Scotch moss agate. You'll find amber, the eons-old
gum from fossils. Genuine amber is precious. You can test it by
rubbing it on wool. This electrifies it and gives it magnetic power.

You'll find cat's-eyes or tiger eyes of Indian quartz, onyx, agate,
turquoise, amethyst, topaz, and garnets, besides the more precious
pearls, diamonds, rubies, and sapphires. Diamonds were usually
rose-cut, meaning they had only twelve facets to give the look of
rose petals. Turquoise may have come from Persia, garnets from
Bohemia, although Brazil, Ceylon, and Burma supplied them, too.
Germany put out a lot of cheap low-karat gold garnet jewelry. A
cabuchon garnet was called a carbuncle. They were also rose-cut,
and garnet-studded pieces of small garnets were some of the most
popular jewelry of the Victorian 1800s.

Besides the gems there were many other kinds of jewelry—fine
carvings of hornbill ivory, enamels on gold, exquisite mosaics
(mostly Italian), tortoise shell, Parian Wedgwood, seed pearls, and
hair. In spite of its macabre source, hair jewelry could be quite
beautiful. Besides being set into rings and lockets, human hair was
woven like fine wire into ropes and balls and bands, even into amusing bangles. But I am told that it does not have a ready sale today
except, perhaps, to the collector.

There was a lot of fine old silver, particularly bracelets of the
coiled serpent type. But the things they did with gold! It was of
course used for the wedding ring, wide and plain or engraved. It
was woven into flexible bands, made into tassels and fringes, into
beads, filigree work, ropes, flat chains called book chains, double-
link chains, and a hollow ware called shellware because it was beaten

over a mold into figures or motifs and backed with a thin layer of the metal. As manufacturers became more numerous and the demand greater, gold jewelry became adulterated and we hear of things like gold-filled, the best of the substitutes, silver-gilt, gold-plate, gold-wash, etc. An English substitute was pinchbeck, not gold at all, but some fine pieces were made of it, and because of its history and rarity it is quite valuable.

What are the pieces you will find? You'll learn that the Victorians liked their jewelry in sets—earrings, pin, bracelets, and necklace. It is said that Queen Elizabeth I originated the idea. You'll find all kinds of rings for men and women. Rings were worn in abundance and on every finger, even the first, and often over the gloves. You might find a posy ring with the initials of the gems spelling a message. Or a gemel or friendship ring of two or more circlets joined by a hand. You'll find signet rings with deep-cut stones for use as seals.

Early Victorian earrings were very large but they were somewhat modified in the later period. Their popularity waned from 1880 to 1900 when the first screw earrings came in. Through history it is a fact that earrings always went out when head coverings came in. Bracelets suffered a setback when sleeves were long. Of course Victorian décolleté made the bracelet popular. Many bracelets were rigid and quite wide, others were flexible with crossed ends. Still others were of flexible mesh or of chains and joined medallions. The dangle bracelet was popular then as now with coins, hearts, etc.

There were all kinds of pins, brooches, shawl pins, scarfpins, cravat pins for the men, belt pins, pins to hold the velvet neck ribbon, bar pins for women.

Chains were decorative in themselves. Watch chains for women were long, so that the watch could be tucked into the belt, although there were shorter "vest" chains for women as well as for men. Old chains are being salvaged for making bracelets or necklaces.

Nothing was more indicative of Victorian sentiment than the locket. Its secrets were jealously guarded. It might hold a lock of hair from a sweetheart or a dead-and-gone loved one or even from a famous personage, a tintype or a small miniature, perhaps a pressed flower. Or maybe only a wad of cotton dipped in perfume which escaped through the pierced back or sides. It was of jet, onyx, shell-gold, inlaid, and sometimes a pin as well as a locket.

Besides all these things you will find many novelties. Among them:

Fobs—From men's watch chains and collected now for bracelets.

Tie Pins—Women are gathering them up and having them combined in sheafs for lapel pins.

Studs and Cuff Links—Both men's and women's. Many attractive ones have come out of the "shirtwaist" era. They make beautiful earrings.

Various Holders—For the handkerchief (attached to a finger ring), for the fan from finger or wrist, for the bouquet, for holding the train while one danced.

A bouquet holder.

Chatelaines—A trinket pin to fasten at the waist on which dangled any number of things such as pencil, memo book, penknife, scissors, matchbox, pin-holder, patch box or powder box, thimble, needlecase, toothpick case, nutmeg grater, a mirror, or a pomander bag, even a dog whistle. Usually of silver.

Hatpins—From the Pompadour period.

Lavalieres—Small pendants of the early 1900s, so called from the famous French beauty, Louise de la Vallière.

Victorian Hands—In many forms from trinkets for hanging on a chain or bracelet to pins and clasps. They had a language like flowers.

Vinaigrettes—Small boxes or figures to hold perfumed cotton. Mid-1800s and earlier.

Smelling Salts—Little gold, silver, or glass phials holding pungent aromatic ammoniac salts for reviving fainting ladies.

Perfume Bottles—A collection of these can go back to Stiegel and South Jersey blown glass. But the little scent bottles that women carried in their gloves or muffs in the gay Nineties are more available, and are bait to the collector.

Perfume bottles and smelling-salts phials.

Watch Cases—Don't worry about the works, but save the cases. They make very interesting pins and compacts.

Chatelaine Pins for Watches—The watch may be gone, but the little gold pin lives on, usually a fleur-de-lis, bowknot, or flower motif. They make fine lapel pins.

Chain Guards—From old watch chains. Being collected and used for bracelet links or charms.

Boxes

Both patch and snuffboxes are important finds. Patch boxes go pretty far back to the beginning of the 1700s, when small patches of black "court plaster" were worn ostensibly to cover a face blemish but also served to advertise a sparkling eye or a flashing dimple. The boxes they were kept in were of metal, possibly Battersea enamel, or of fine china like Bow, Chelsea, or Staffordshire. They are decidedly collectors' pieces and museum stuff. Snuffboxes, however, come closer to home. They were used as late as the end of Grant's administration. Early ones were of tin, pewter, horn, or papier-mâché. Many had paper prints of historical subjects or of the presidents upon them. All are collectibles.

Fans

Here is where most collectors go wild—and I don't blame them. The fan, at its best, is a work of art comparable to a fine painting. Although fans go back to biblical times, the first fans were brought to Europe by the Chinese. The Japanese are said to have originated the folding fan. Medieval fans were disk-shaped, flag fans or tufts of plumes. Italian fans were made of vellum, paper, or swan's skin, the mounts beautifully painted on both sides, blades with gold or silver inlay or gem-studded mother-of-pearl. In France, the blades were of carved ivory, tortoise shell, or mother-of-pearl, often telling a story of knights and ladies. Less expensive fan sticks were of sandalwood or fruit wood. Both Flanders and Italy had lace fans. In Spain, vellum was mounted on imported sticks and painted by famous artists. These old fans of kid or lambskin beaten to silken softness are called "chicken skin."

On some of the old fans mirrors were set into the sticks, and in Spain a fan was turned into a mask by having eye slits cut into the mount. In the seventeenth and eighteenth centuries French fan mountings were designed by such famous artists as Watteau, Boucher, and Fragonard. Lacquer gave them the look of fine enamel.

In time many of these fans reached America. By 1732 fans were being made in great numbers in Philadelphia and Boston. The finer sticks were still imported, but wooden sticks were made here and painted. From 1830 to 1860 America had plenty of its own fans, made of paper, painted, turkey feathers, sandalwood, etc. Southern belles preferred brise or minuet fans with carved blades of ivory, mother-of-pearl, or sandalwood, and no mounts. The autograph fan flourished from 1863 to 1890. Chinese fans were popular in this country, the plain fan often being made here and sent over to China for embellishment. In the nineteenth century the mourning fan, with dark sticks of smoked pearl, ebony, or jet, was a costume asset.

Many of us can remember the ostrich fan and the spangled net or chiffon fan of the early 1900s. There are still many of these around, although they are beginning to be novelties, too. There are also lace fans of Brussels rose point, some appliquéd on net with spangles or marcasite set into dark tortoise sticks. Black and white lace fans were the mode up to 1900.

These are the fine ones to look out for. But there are many others. It might be amusing to collect just those carrying an advertising legend.

Bride's Boxes, Bandboxes, and Bonnet Boxes

Quaint peasant-decorated boxes of thin wood were imported from Bavaria and Switzerland by the Pennsylvania Dutch and probably made by them, too. They were called bride's boxes—a present from the groom on or before his wedding day for his bride's finery. You might be lucky enough to own one or find one. Bandboxes were designed to hold small dress accessories such as neckbands, sashes, ribbons, etc. Both these and the bonnet boxes—sometimes called Hannah Davis boxes after the New Hampshire woman who sold them—were of thin wood or cardboard and covered with wallpaper. They are sought today as much for the wallpaper designs as for anything else, also for the old newspapers with which they were lined. Men's hatboxes, if not of leather, were also paper-covered. If you come across one with a printed paper showing balloons, railroads, or canal boats you can count yourself lucky.

Combs

It is said the first factory for combs in America was established at Newbury, Massachusetts, in 1759, making combs for general use only. Ornamental combs of ivory, tortoise shell, and horn came into use about 1773. I happen to know personally of an early comb business conducted by one of my own forebears in Pennsylvania near Reading, a Charles Michael Crouse who came to this country in 1758. He later became an officer in Washington's army and is said to have made combs of cattle horn for the troops at Valley Forge. The cattle horn was boiled, pressed into flat sheets, and worked by hand. I have seen and played with some of the family combs carved like the fine Spanish shell combs. But unfortunately the worms got into my heritage and they are no longer around to tell the tale. The instruments that made them are reposing in the Bucks County Museum at Doylestown, Pennsylvania. Today a seventh generation is still making combs but with machinery.

Buttons

Here is a subject big enough to fill many books. Button collectors are perhaps the most fervent in the world, and they have wide sources to pull from. Until you have leafed through one of the big button books you will have no idea of how many different kinds of buttons there can be. Several things can be said of button collecting: the supply is good, except in rare instances, there are not many reproductions, and the prices won't wreck the budget. I shall attempt to list only a few varieties, enough to set you thinking and looking through your button box or on your "charm string." (You know what that was—a string of 999 buttons, each different—an achievement in casual collecting.)

Buttons have been made of every conceivable substance: gold, silver, brass, copper, pewter, cut steel, jeweled, set with brilliants and rhinestones; hand painted on porcelain, or decorated with transfer pictures; satsuma, Battersea enamel, ivory, horn, tortoise shell, inlay, Wedgwood cameo, cloisonné, Delft, rubber, wood, crystal, carved and smoked pearls, colored, pressed, and lacy glass, lithographed under glass or celluloid, reverse-painted on glass, papier-mâché, tapestry, cameo, opal, satin under glass, jet, swirled glass like the paperweights and marbles. Have I left anything out?

You can collect uniform buttons, heraldric emblems, fans, hands, zodiac signs, coins, masks, clocks, Indians, dogs, cats, horses, deer, reptiles, fish, shells, marine life, fabulous animals, birds, insects, flowers, fruits, operatic buttons, theatrical buttons, famous women, sweethearts, buildings, transportation, biblical characters, fables, nursery rhymes, children's stories, history, sports, mythology, cupids, fairies, calico patterns—I could go on for pages.

Why are buttons so picturesque and so plentiful? For many years they were used strictly for ornament. The buttons left on a man's suit sleeve are a holdover from that time. Many religious sects even today do not use buttons because they are too "worldly." A button was often a token given to a sweetheart, and today it can make a good friend if she happens to be a button collector. Dates to remember about American buttons: the first covered wooden button came into use in 1826, the invention of a woman in East Hampshire, Massachusetts. Pearl buttons were made about 1885. Get out the button box!

Shawls

In 1798 the French and English troops in Egypt were smitten by the beautiful Oriental shawls they saw, and brought or sent them home to their wives from Egypt, Persia, and Turkey. Thus the fashion began. An Indian cashmere shawl was not cheap, even then. Because of narrow looms, it was woven in several pieces but joined almost invisibly. From 1820 to 1870 these shawls imported to France were the vogue, 3½ yards long, 1½ yards wide, some square, with woven or embroidered borders. They were often made double so they could be reversed.

The Paisley shawl was an effort to reproduce something for those who could not afford the cashmere shawl, not an imitation, but a substitute. Paisley shawls were made in Paisley, Scotland, in the familiar Persian cone pattern in four or five colors, woven in one piece, the colors reversed on the back. By 1834 the shawl business in England and America ran to $5,000,000 a year. By 1850 shawls were top fashion. The printed shawl and the plaid shawl followed. Men wore them. By 1870 shawls had gone quite fancy and were made of silk or lace, heavily fringed.

Don't throw out even a small bit of Paisley or cashmere. Cut away the moth-eaten parts and save the best of it for a purse or the border of a table runner or cushion top. They were both beautiful bits of weaving.

Umbrellas and Parasols

It isn't likely you will want to use an old umbrella or parasol except for theatricals. But the handles may be worth saving. They are being collected. Umbrellas in America go back to 1772 and had wooden frames. Early ones had acorns for handles because the acorn was thought to be a talisman against lightning. Steel frames came in about 1850. In the mid-1800s parasols were quite small—a style traced to Napoleon's Josephine. They were called carriage parasols and could be tilted against the sun. Some were quite flat, some pagoda-shaped. Like the fan, the parasol was a coquette's standby.

Bureau Novelties

All the bureau trinkets have good reason for being saved. To list them briefly: trinket boxes, powder boxes, trays of glass, china, and milk glass, pin boxes (particularly those small china furniture miniatures with lids—bureaus, pianos, etc.), ring trees, hatpin holders, matched sets of stoppered glass bottles with trays or boxes, pincushions, etc.

Costume Accessories and Clothes

These things from old trunks pose a problem. There are some costume collectors who will welcome anything in the way of dress, but unless they are very old I would suggest donating them to a little-theater group who will be glad to have them for costume plays. There are a few exceptions to be kept in mind, things like old reticules or misers' purses of beadwork or petit point should be treated with respect, also handkerchiefs, the old printed ones, particularly those dating back to the 1830s and often commemorating a historical event or a presidential campaign. Children's handkerchiefs with nursery rhymes are collectibles, too. Gloves, mitts, shoes, snoods, fichus, scarves, all have value for someone, and are better given to those who appreciate them than sold to the junkman.

17. TOYS, MINIATURES, AND BANKS

THIS is a field where the collector can run riot. I can't imagine anyone setting out to buy old toys or iron banks unless he or she has the idea of starting or adding to a collection. However, I can understand the desire to hold on to old playthings you might find in the family treasures for sentimental reasons. If what you should happen to find has no personal associations and no artistic appeal—as many toys do not—I would suggest getting rid of it to the highest bidder.

Dolls, perhaps, are an exception. It is easy to fall in love with an old doll without any intention of becoming one of the hundreds of doll collectors in this country. Or it may be a temptation to pick up several dolls for display on your shelves and, if you know what you are buying, it might well be a good investment. The doll demand grows and widens, and prices rise accordingly. There are a number of good books written on dolls with which it would be a good idea to check. Of course not all doll collectors go in exclusively for antique dolls, but if this is your idea it might be well to narrow down your selections to dates or kinds.

Among the old dolls that you will find today many will not be of

American origin. Germany and France both supplied this country with dolls for many years, even after manufacture started here. Dolls, incidentally, were not always toys. They were used for religious purposes, for processions, crèches, etc., and were often only miniature fashion models. The word "doll" is supposed to have been used for the first time in England in 1751. Old books call dolls puppets.

Dolls have been made of many materials—wood, rag, wax, papiermâché, china, bisque, leather, rubber, celluloid, and plastics, but in this country until 1800 they were of wood, often carved by fond fathers or local craftsmen. Wooden heads with stuffed bodies of kid or cloth did not come into the picture until after 1800. One of the most primitive of dolls was the cornhusk doll, possibly borrowed from the Indian children, although it has been found through the South even in more recent years. In those early days a little girl's imagination could endow her piece of wood or cornhuskings wrapped in a cotton cloth with the beauty of fine bisque.

Also homemade and primitive were the rag dolls with button eyes and wool hair like the Raggedy Ann and Andy brought out many years later. This stuffed rag toy is a truly American institution. It was revived in the 1890s with printed muslin patterns to be stuffed at home, many of which were animals. One doll in this cuddly toy class has an interesting history—the Teddy bear. It has been called the boys' doll. It was made by a bedridden German woman, maker of soft toys, on order from an American buyer who suggested some kind of doll based on Teddy Roosevelt and his bear-shooting sorties. She evolved the Teddy bear and started something that made big business history. One firm alone is reported as making 4,000,000 in the span of twenty-five years.

The first realistic composition head for a doll was made in America by Ludwig Greiner of Philadelphia in 1858. It was a sort of papier-mâché. He made heads only, and the date, when marked, can be found inside the head. Most heads made after 1872 bear the date. A Greiner doll means a find to a collector.

There was a man in Vermont, Joel Ellis, whose name also means a lot in the doll world. He made an articulated wooden doll with knife joints, commercializing it in 1873. Another doll of the period, called a Martin doll, had a hemispherical joint at the shoulders.

China and porcelain dolls have been attributed to the English Staffordshire potters, but most of them came from Germany from a town named Sonneburg, long a center of the toy industry. France, too, sent over fine Parian and bisque heads with molded hair, jewels, dress ruchings, etc. The best known of these is the Jumeau doll of about 1862. In this country the Fulper Pottery of Flemington, New Jersey, made doll heads of bisque, although they could not approach the imported ones. Just recently old bisque Fulper heads, made in Flemington from 1918 to 1921, are being advertised.

For a long time dolls were made "movable" by stitching the cloth or leather at the knees and elbows, later by ball-and-socket joints and by stringing them with rubber or wires. One way to tell the age of a doll is by the character of the stitching, as machine stitching did not come in until 1850. Another way to tell the age of a china head is by the number of holes used to stitch it to the soft body. Older dolls had only one hole front and back, later ones two holes. All dolls brought into the United States after 1892 had to have the name of the exporting country on them. There are books of doll trademarks that may help to determine origin.

Up until 1900 most dolls were grownups, with few baby dolls. The lady doll of the period from 1860 to 1890 was a fashionable creature whether she was made of china, bisque, or wax, with perhaps real eyelashes and hair set hair by hair into the wax. (Famous wax dolls were the Italian Montanari and the English Pierotti, covering a span from 1790 to 1935.) Sometimes the doll had closing eyes that worked on a weight, or maybe a mechanism for walking. A doll of the early 1900s sought by collectors is the Schoenhut wooden doll made by the toy firm in Philadelphia.

Novelty dolls of the late 1800s included talking dolls that said Mama and Papa and sang songs from hidden phonographs with sets of records. There were also mechanical dolls who did various tricks, such as playing a fiddle, riding a bicycle, or preaching from a pulpit. They were showpieces but are now collectors' items. There were two-faced dolls with heads that turned (Jumeau) and "comb" dolls of rubber, so called because made by the India Rubber Comb Company in 1851. There were squeak dolls and tumbling dolls with marbles inside. There were many "penny" dolls, the tiny ones, made for the small home dressmaker or for doll houses. Once you start on this fascinating hobby there is no end to what you may find. Paper dolls are a big collectible item, too. They are not as new as they might seem. It is said that the French court of Louis XVI used them, manipulating them with strings and giving them words by ventriloquism to parody existing personalities. The first American paper doll was Jenny Lind (1850), equipped with ten of the costumes she wore in her operatic roles. There were plenty of paper soldiers and Indians. *Godey's Lady's Book* in 1859 ran a series of paper-doll cutouts. Many paper-doll strips were given away as advertising items for things such as ONT cotton, Willimantic Thread Company, Lion Coffee Company's doll house, and the Aunt Jemima pancake flour doll which was brought out in both paper and rag and persisted for years.

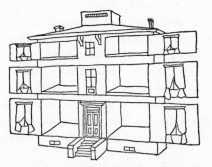

The front walls of this Georgian doll house open like doors.

From dolls it is a short step to doll houses. Here we overlap into the domain of the miniature collectors, because so many of the "tinies," as they were often called, were made expressly for doll houses as well as for oddities and displays of skill. There are a number of famous doll houses often put on display for charity, such as Queen Mary's doll house in England, Titania's Palace in Canada, Mrs. Thorne's Miniature Period Rooms, to name a few. But the story of doll houses does not stop there. Many were homemade by loving hands. Often rooms were housed in cupboards with divided shelves, with glass or solid doors. Sometimes they were barns, cottages, or castles. Always they are entrancing if only for the collections of the period furniture and accessories made to the proper scale. The exclamation always is, "How do they do it?"

Many well-known people have gone in for miniaturia, such as Jack Norworth the actor, Colleen Moore, Helena Rubenstein, and Jules Charbneau, who is said to have gathered 28,000 items in fifty years of collecting, all of which could be carried in one small trunk and a suitcase. But there is nothing to stop you and me from starting such a collection. Just the other day I was allowed behind the scenes in the house of a dealer I know well who showed me her private collection built up since she was a little girl, probably not more than twenty-five years ago. It included besides two doll houses filled with pieces, doll furniture and china, and a whole cabinet of Pennsylvania Dutch red-clay and copper utensils few more than an inch high. The collection literally filled one small bedroom. It can be done, not so easily as formerly, of course. Don't be caught, however, by trash just because it is small. Tiny things demand the finest in craftsmanship. There are people who have given up their lives to making these reproductions in miniature, some do it for a hobby, but I am always amazed at the skill involved.

All old toys are of interest if they have any claim to age, novelty, or rarity. I think perhaps a list here will be sufficient to make you aware of what is being sought and send you scurrying to your attics.

Doll's Furniture—From the primitive, homemade pieces to the fine period piece. Cradles are particularly good.

Doll's Dishes—These were often of the same imported china as the family pieces, Gaudy Dutch, Staffordshire transfer, ironstone, etc. Tea sets came in Britannia ware about 1875. Pressed-glass sets and cruet stands will turn up. Some of these were salesmen's samples not made primarily as toys, but undoubtedly they fell into the hands of delighted little girls.

Iron Play Stoves and Pots and Pans—Very popular now though not so old.

Pianos—That played an octave or two. The Schoenut is a good example.

Doll Carriages—An American product from 1868 to 1875. Styles vary with the period, from prams to gocarts.

Toy Stores—Butcher shops, grocery stores, dry-goods emporiums, also things like "tin kitchens," of which an old one dates from 1790.

A toy iron stove.

Soldiers—All kinds, wood, cardboard, paper (after 1820), lead, and even "sugar." A specialized hobby. Whole shops are given over to supplying the collectors of this item.

Guns—All kinds with an emphasis on the cap pistols first made in 1876. Much in demand.

Marbles—Early ones were crude, of clay, glass, or stone, but later ones from 1833 to late 1800s very showy. Include sulphides, onyx, jade, jasper, carnelian, Venetian swirls.

Tops—An old toy in America used in the seventeenth and eighteenth centuries as well as the nineteenth and twentieth.

Hobbyhorses—Of many kinds, the horse on a wheeled platform, the rocking horse, horse in a frame or combined with a bicycle. Earliest ones were crude, hand-whittled from pine, legs merely suggested, occasionally painted. Pony-skin covering, bridles, etc., came in later. Made in this country in quantity from 1840 to 1890. Include here other animals which could be ridden. Also the merry-go-round horse.

Jumping Jacks and Jack-in-the-boxes—Old and not so old.

Noah's Arks—Particularly those with the hand-carved animals. Also hand-carved *putz* (Pennsylvania Dutch) figures for Christmas crèche or village.

Pull Toys—A great favorite with collectors, not only the mechanical ones of wood or tin, but those of iron like early fire engines, trains, boats, horse and wagons, etc.

Whistles—Particularly the ceramic bird whistles.

Sand Toys—Many were made between 1855 and 1875.

Magic Lanterns—Both the lanterns and boxes of slides have value.

Zoetropes—And other similar "moving-picture" toys, where a strip of pictures of figures is pulled past a series of openings to give a semblance of motion.

Toy Theaters—If you can find one with pasteboard characters, scenery, and script of a play you are lucky.

Old Picture Books—A specialized subject. Take them to an old book dealer. The *Kate Greenaway ABC* book very desirable, also old Mother Goose books.

A pull-toy elephant to be ridden.

Christmas Tree Ornaments—These are in demand. Many were German. Of wax, plaster, or unglazed pottery, tinseled pictures, spun glass, etc. Date from about 1850. Fine old German balls are worth saving. Japanese ornaments came in about 1920. Blown-glass ornaments go back to the 1700s. Christmas-tree lights of colored glass to shield the candles are among sought-for glass pieces. Often quite valuable.

Easter Baskets and Eggs—Decorated eggs, especially engraved or "scratched" eggs, should be saved. With care they last for years. Don't overlook the egg with the peephole and a scene inside.

Abacus—The old counting frame with balls. You'll find one once in a while.

Slates—Old school slates in good condition get rarer and rarer. They bring good prices now.

Outdoor Toys—Velocipedes, sleds, wagons, and pull carriages. Not too many around of the older kind, but don't ignore them.

Banks—Still and Mechanical

A few years ago the antique shops always had a few banks on hand, both kinds, the ones that worked when a penny was deposited and the ones that were stationary. They lingered on the shelves until the word got around that mechanical banks were being collected, then prices soared, and now a good mechanical bank is almost a rarity. Interest has only recently moved on to the stepchild, the still bank. Now they, too, are being collected and bring good prices. Both of these banks are not yet one hundred years old. The oldest dates from about 1869. They were made until about 1900. While the moving bank was designed to teach thrift by giving a child a show for his money, there is no doubt that it became a race for ingeniousness on the part of the makers. These banks have a sort of custard-pie, slapstick humor often with political overtones.

Left, a William Tell mechanical bank. *Right,* a Columbine and Harlequin mechanical bank.

Scarcity has put the prices of some of these banks to unbelievable heights. A Harlequin and Columbine, of which only a few exist, has gone as high as $3,000. Collectors in the know can tell you just about how many there are in the rare models, yet often they are fooled when another one turns up unexpectedly. I was instrumental in bringing to light a Sewing Machine bank for a collector friend who had said there were only nine he knew of in existence, and he knew where they were. I found the tenth. When a collection is broken up and goes on the market, there is a scurrying among the buyers. They are more likely to swap pieces among themselves than to sell outright. All in all, it is an exciting hobby. Some of the better-known banks are: Kicking Cow, Dentist, Ferris Wheel, Skipping Rope, Professor Pug-Frog, William Tell, Girl in the Victorian Chair, Presto, the Fowler, and the Breadwinner, to name only a few. As for the still banks, look for such things as Black Beauty, Mutt and Jeff, and the Flatiron Building.

If you come upon an iron bank, even if not in working condition, regard it highly, and make inquiries about your nearest collector. Your local antique dealer will probably know who it is.

Children's Gift Mugs and Plates

Children's mugs are an important item among collectors. They are quaint and amusing and often fine examples of the ceramic styles of their day. Thus you will find in a good collection luster,

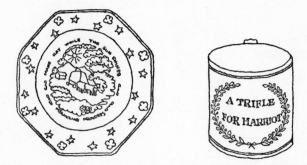

Left, a Franklin maxim gift plate. *Right,* a Victorian child's gift mug.

canary, Gaudy Dutch, ironstone, and marked pieces from Leeds, Liverpool, and Bristol. Many are transfer printed. They were the gift mugs of the nineteenth century, a personalized gift for children from Auntie or Grandma. On them you will find many first names such as Charles, Philip, William, James, and John; Sara, Cynthia, Isabella, Sophia, Eliza, and Harriet—a far cry from the Sandras, Lindas, and Dianes of today. If the name was not available, Auntie could always find one "For a Good Girl" or "A Present for My Favorite." There were reward mugs inscribed "For Loving a Book," "For Knitting Well," "For Going to School" or "For Writing Well." Transfer pictures showed games and sports such as seesaw, marbles, shuttlecock, and pegtop, and the scenes from old nursery tales. There were motto mugs with an inscription such as, *Idleness Brings Disgrace,* Kate Greenaway mugs, alphabet mugs, and animal mugs. One old collection of note is said to have included 1,200 mugs. I know of one personally that numbers well over one hundred.

The story of children's plates follows much the same pattern. They, too, were made for "good children" from 1820 to 1870, and include the markings of some of the best Staffordshire potters such as Clews and from Swansea in Wales. The most popular is the ABC plate, sometimes of tin, but more often of earthenware with the letters in an embossed border and occasionally colored. The centers of these plates could be almost anything, an illustrated Franklin maxim such as "Let's make hay while the sun shines," or a riddle plate with the question on the front and the answer on the back. There were pictures of Civil War heroes, a series of Uncle Tom's cabin plates, and a set of Robinson Crusoe plates. They taught the children to say their prayers, virtues like temperance and industry, geography and history. Any antique dealer will give more than a cursory glance at one of these plates.

PART III

If You Are Going to Buy Antiques

18. HOW TO START

YOU have just come from a talk at the women's club where an expert has held forth on cup plates or old pewter or old fans. Or your husband has heard a man speak at the Rotary on Kentucky rifles. You are both fired with the fact that old things can be beautiful, valuable, and adaptable to your modern way of life. Or your best friend has done over her country house entirely in "primitives" and it has turned into a homey, attractive place for year-round living. Or you're a bride-to-be and you've just seen a picture of a kitchen spiked up with all kinds of old things on the shelves and walls and around the fireplace and you want one just like it. Or perhaps, now that the children have grown up, you are about to refurnish the living room but you aren't drawn to the modern. So you decide to acquire some antiques. How do you go about it, assuming you know nothing about buying them?

It's a good idea to have at least a smattering of knowledge before you start out. Read a few general books on antiques—I have listed some in the bibliography. Or leaf over the antique magazines at your library, or buy a few copies at any good news agency. Go to shows and auction sales before you start buying seriously. You may break down and pick up a cracked sugarbowl for a song, or a silly little souvenir mug from Niagara Falls for a dollar. But that won't matter. You have to begin somewhere, and it will always be a conversation piece. "That's the first antique I ever bought," you'll say. "It started me off." Just don't buy the first silver tea set or grandfather's clock you see. A good friend who knows her way around in the antique world is a fine thing to have in these first days.

You'll probably do your first buying in a shop. Now antique buying is not like department-store buying. You'll have to shop around because what you buy will be conditioned by what you can find. But you must know what to ask for. You won't feel nearly so awkward and ignorant if you can ask for a slope-front desk or a harvest table or a butterfly Windsor when you walk into a shop. Just don't try to appear more knowing than you are. Be honest with the dealer. He'll respect you for it and will put himself out to help you.

You'll undoubtedly start by "just looking." The antique business being what it is, dealers expect a lot of looking. But they like to think it isn't entirely idle browsing, that you have *intentions* of buying. Right here I'd like to mention some of the things that can make you a thorn in the flesh of a patient dealer. Good manners are just as necessary in an antique shop as anywhere else.

First, don't turn into a Professional Looker. Dealers abhor the Lookers who must be treated as courteously as Buyers because they may just possibly break down and buy. They are the window-shoppers of the antique business, the ones who "antique" for something to do, who like to compare prices disparagingly and talk glibly about antiques without reading the books or spending their money, who can't pass a shop without going in to browse. It's an occupational hazard that turns shopkeepers gray and sour. To have to hover first on one foot then the other for an hour while a listless Looker goes through the stock is hard on the patience. It's a good plan to announce what you are looking for when you first enter a shop, so the dealer will know your visit is not a purely idle one, or at least to ask if you may look around, and apologize for taking up time if you don't buy.

A form of Looker is known in the trade as a Lidlifter. This is the person who goes around the shop handling everything, lifting lids for no reason except that he or she has itchy fingers. It's the man who whips out his penknife to scratch away the paint to see the wood—and perhaps doesn't recognize one wood from another. Unless you need to feel for texture, resonance, chips, etc., don't handle the stock. Let the dealer do it for you.

This brings up the question of breaking. No one intentionally breaks things in a shop, of course, but it is easy to grab a cracked teapot handle, or sit on a wobbly chair, or swing a shoulder bag against a shelf, or let a bulky coat brush against a tableful of glass. Some dealers post a warning sign, *Handle at Your Own Risk,* but sign or no sign, good manners should prompt you to make good any loss that is your fault. It's so easy to be a bull in a crowded, antique china shop. Once I saw a child at an antique show, being trundled behind his casual, carefree young mother in a small cart, put out a hand to grab a tablecloth and yank a whole tableful of dishes to the floor. Someone else caught him just in time, and all his mother said was "Oh!" I wonder if she would have or could have paid for the damage. Children have no place in a shop full of breakables.

Don't, *please* don't cry out when you see a familiar piece, "Look at this! Five dollars! Why, I just threw out one just like it. It belonged to my grandmother, and she got it free with a pound of baking powder, I know she did. Five dollars! It's robbery!" Then in a whisper, "I bet *she*"—with a look for the dealer—"didn't pay five cents for it." I know it's hard to restrain yourself in the presence of these things within our memories which have just become antiques but the dealers hate it. It casts aspersions on their stock and it makes them feel like highwaymen. Maybe the dealer did pay only five cents for it or fifty cents or one dollar, but the current market price in the shops is five dollars, and she is entitled to her piece of good luck.

Don't be what the dealers call the Suspicious Ones. They have an antagonistic attitude that is apparent the minute they enter a shop. They clutch their handbags, they talk in whispers, they are sure they are going to be "taken." Now it is well to be on the alert, but until a dealer is proved to be sharp or dishonest, give him the benefit of the doubt. The antique business today is a reputable one, far removed from the shoddy outgrowth of the junk heap. Knowing people have gone into it—I wouldn't be surprised to hear of courses in antiques being given in colleges soon. Certainly a lot of history can be learned from its study. Dealers' associations keep check now on the fly-by-night or unscrupulous trader. If you have doubts about the standing of a strange dealer, consult a local Chamber of Commerce or Better Business Bureau or bank or ask his neighbors. You'll hear gossip about most dealers, as you will in any business, but if you ask *enough* questions from both interested and disinterested people you can probably get the true picture.

Don't feel offended if a dealer keeps some of his things under lock and key. You may be honest, but how does he know? There are many kleptomaniacs as well as real thieves going the rounds of the shops. Don't be offended if he refuses to take a check. A dishonest buyer can be hundreds of miles away before the dealer finds the check is worthless.

Don't dicker. The most reliable dealers will usually price their items plainly and stick to their prices. Some will come down if they need quick cash or feel that in doing so they are making a good new customer. Others display no prices at all—a habit to be suspected although it may only be a form of snobbishness, as if to say, "What does the price matter for a fine thing like this?" But it may mean that it gives them a chance to come down or go up, according to how they size up the customer. Generally speaking, I always feel more comfortable and more like dealing with a shop that displays its prices. I know where I stand, and I don't have to bother the owner every minute asking, "How much is this?" Of course there are dealers who are out to get as much as the shopper will put up.

I am reminded here of a funny old gentleman in my neighborhood who has a sprawling place, more of a junk shop than an antique shop, but because he is situated in a part of the country where there are still good things in hiding, his stock will come up very often with some good pieces. But his ideas of prices are ridiculous. I have never been able to figure out how he arrives at them. Is he ignorant or just canny? He follows no market pattern. And so what happens? We spar good-naturedly, and I come off with what I want at a considerably lower figure, but I wonder if there are some ignorant ones who pay his first price and if he banks on that?

There is another shop I know up near the Canadian border, a big house with sheds and barns chuck full of fine things and some not so fine. Prices are high. The first thing I spotted there on my first visit was a weatherbeaten comb-back Windsor on the porch.

The indifferent dealer gave me a price which I finally took, a little stiff but not exorbitant. Later I learned that he always cut his prices when he found out you were actually out to buy or had made several purchases. I was always sorry I had acted so quickly on that chair. I'd have got it much cheaper if I had waited.

A word of caution, however: don't be a pest about asking for a better price. Most dealers hate it. If the piece you covet seems too high—or at least for your pocketbook—say so regretfully rather than critically and let the dealer come down if he wants to. You'd be surprised how often a dealer likes to see the "right" person own a fine piece that he himself prizes. And as for the dealer's discount, which usually runs from 10 per cent to 20 per cent and is a courtesy mark-off in the trade, don't ask for it, even though you may have "dealt" privately with a few friends. Usually a dealer expects some kind of proof that you are a fellow dealer, a card or a letterhead. So don't try it.

A word about returning things. Some dealers are most co-operative about letting things go out of the shop on approval, but if you are not well known to him, this is asking too much. Many will not allow it, because they have been stung too often with damaged articles returned to them, with sales lost while they were out of the shop, and so on. But most of them will hold their things for you if you put down a deposit on them. It isn't fair to ask a dealer to hold anything even for a few hours without a deposit, and when he does accept a deposit, it is well to say when you will come for it. He can't hold things forever. But this procedure does give you time to go home and measure and speculate before you complete the purchase.

So now you are primed, and you've learned your way around the shops. One thing to remember is the matter of delivery if you can't take your purchase with you. Some dealers will deliver gratis. Most leave it up to you, or charge for expressage and crating. So consider this extra charge before you buy. At an auction sale it is up to you to get the piece off the premises.

Your next best source of finding antiques is the auction sale. Before an auction sale starts you'll probably hear the "terms" of sale announced, but there are other things to know if you have not made a habit of going to sales. It takes courage to bid if you are not used to it. Be sure to speak up loud and get the auctioneer's attention, but don't wave your hands or make wild gestures unless you are bidding or you may find a horrible umbrella stand has just been knocked down to you for $10. Sit up front, so you can see and hear and be heard. Later, when you get real adept at all the tricks of bidding, it may help to keep as inconspicuous as possible. One macabre old man I meet at sales never says a word, does it all with the droop of his left eyelid. I always watch him closely.

It behooves you to look over the things to be sold before the sale begins. Go early enough to make a tour of the things displayed and note down what you want and the limit you are prepared to pay for it—if you know. Sometimes, when the sale is large and important, you can examine the pieces the day before and can leave a bid for what you want if you can't attend the sale.

It is easy to get carried away at a sale. Make up your mind to be resolute when a coveted piece begins to move away from you. Some sales employ bidders to up the prices and egg you on. Be canny about jumping in quickly with a low bid; you just might get it. Be canny, too, at jumping in at the end when two are battling for the piece. Sometimes a fresh bidder discourages them and they give up. Be sure you are not bidding against your husband or your best friend. Enemies have been made in this way.

Bargains are usually picked up in the early hours before the crowds come and late in the day when people begin to go home, or just before they wander off for lunch. Of course the auctioneer will not put up the important items at these times, but I have picked up many a nice tidbit when nobody was paying much attention. If you are in a hurry, you can often get an auctioneer to put up something you've been waiting for before he gets around to it.

Let's suppose this is your first sale and you've never bid before. It's a good idea to make a "practice run" with something not too important. Listen carefully to the auctioneer. When he says, "Who'll give me five dollars for this fine old platter?" you know nobody will —at first. So you pipe up, "Fifty cents." Maybe he'll laugh, but don't let that disturb you. Someone else will say, "One dollar," and the bidding is on. If you really want it, come back with "One and a quarter." Now you can usually tell if the figure bid is low or high by the activity or pace of the bidding. If it is a good buy, the bids are fast and furious, overlapping each other. Maybe this is the time for you to get out, especially if you don't know how high to go. Just wait and watch and listen and record the price for future bargaining. But if the bidding is sluggish, you may get the platter without much opposition. Maybe it is not a readily salable item for the dealers, just possibly no one recognizes its worth, or there have been a lot of platters already sold that day. So you get the platter for a dollar and a quarter—and you find it has a crack through the rim. Oh well, it's not a bad one, and it *is* pretty! But the next time you'll be sure you are bidding on a perfect piece.

How do you know what to bid? Many people don't. You can pick out someone who seems to know what it's all about and watch him. Or you put out a feeler and see how far it goes. As you get more familiar with current prices, you won't have to guess. But at first you jump in like a kid with a grab bag and see what you can get. I once had a friend whom we called the Ten-center. She was always on hand with a ten-cent bid and strangely enough she picked up many a nice little item for that price. So have I in the old days. Today, you can't go far even with a quarter.

Don't try to outbid the dealers. Most of them know exactly what they can get in their shops for what they are bidding on, and some of them even have customers waiting for certain things, and so they can afford to carry the bid fairly high. And don't get strung along by a moneyed bidder who has no idea of worth but is willing to pay anything to get the gold-framed mirror or the cute doll's cradle. You'd better drop out of such a fray and let her have it.

How do you know where to find sales? Every large city has one or more auction rooms which usually advertise. Country sales are advertised in local papers. Some antique-minded people subscribe to several country papers for that purpose. Here's a sample ad for a sale:

Extra Large Sale

OF ANTIQUES, FARM MACHINERY, TOOLS, ETC., Saturday, October 20th, at 10 A.M. on Route 322, 6 miles north of Downingtown, 6 miles south of Honeybrook near Brandywine Manor Church.

HOUSEHOLD GOODS—3 Grandfathers clocks, 2 corner cupboards, walnut Welsh cupboard, 2 slant top desks, 2 dry sinks,

2 jelly cupboards, 15 marble top tables of all kinds, coffee table, marble top washstands & bureaus, 6 chests of drawers, 8 blanket chests, 6 drop-leaf tables, 3 cradles, side boards, sofas, Hepplewhite love seat, chairs (fireside, half spindle, ladderback, Windsor, etc.), miniature settee, wood boxes, mirrors and some good modern furniture. 35 old and modern guns, swords, old Banks China (Gaudy Welsh, Ironstone, Haviland, majolica, etc.), GLASS—thumbprint, pressed & cut, old clocks, old picture frames, old fireplace fixtures; iron, brass & copper kettles, sleigh bells. Very old organ in good condition.

MACHINERY—Blizzard ensilage cutter, 2-bottom J. D. plow, side delivery rake, dump rake, wagons, lot of tools, log chains, block & tackle, bolts, some good sash & doors, many other articles too numerous to mention. 60-ton of mixed hay, and pony & saddle. This sale must start promptly at 10 A.M.

    Machinery & Tools at 10 A.M.

    Household goods at 11 A.M.

                                Morris Speakman, Owner

H. E. Funderwhite, Sales Mgr.

J. M. Seltzer, Auct.

Humpton & Paxon, Clerks.

    Lunch by Civic Assoc. of Brandywine Twp.

Smaller sales will sometimes put up a notice in the local post office. These are the sales to watch for, because they do not draw the crowds and among the crocks and old tools there might be just one fine piece to be had cheap. Most sales are held in the spring and fall and on Saturdays. You can spot them as you ride through the countryside by the lineup of cars along the road. Some sales are slated for the long summer evenings, some are regular once-a-month sales in halls or auction rooms. In some parts of the country there is a growing custom of Friday-night markets where everything is sold, even antiques.

It's a good idea to get yourself put on the list of a big auction room for advance notices of important sales. One of the country's finest collection of bottles and flasks was recently sold not too far from me in a big auction house. I paid a dollar for the catalogue in advance and at the sale jotted down prices against the items as a fine reference book on values for old bottles.

I've never come across any phony sales. Some auctioneers are better than others, however. Some know what they are selling, some don't, some will take back a piece that has been found to be defective and put it up again, some go through a sale at a breakneck pace selling everything and letting the buyer beware. But all in all they are honest.

Sales are fun even if you come home with a ten-cent toothpick holder or a broken parasol.

Your next source of supply is the antique show. Here you have the advantage of looking over the selected stock of many dealers, but on the other hand you will not see all that they have. However, if you want something special ask about it and you may find they have just what you need back home in the shop. Just the other day I was helping a friend to buy a bench table. There was one at a local show, but when I went to look at it for her it had been sold. I happened to mention it to another dealer I knew and found out that she had a better one and at a lower price at home. I told my friend, and her search was ended. The tracking down of good things is always a challenge and fun no matter how you do it.

But do take it slowly. Don't go haywire and buy the first bed you see or a rare fairy lamp when what you need is a good chest for the hall. If I were going to start furnishing with antiques, I'd buy one piece at a time, putting myself on a budget and getting along with the minimum, mixing it with what I already have until the modern has all been replaced with the old. I'd begin with such pieces as a fine desk, a corner cupboard, a drop-leaf table, a chest of drawers. Things that can be shifted around until your program is complete. Shopping around pays off. I hate to quote prices because they can change overnight, but be prepared to pay enough to get good authentic pieces. Leave the astronomically priced rare pieces for the connoisseurs. Figure at least $100 for a finished drop-leaf table, $165 to $185 for a pine harvest or Lazy Susan table, $225 for a six-leg cherry table, $100 to $125 for a plain pine corner cupboard, as high as $400 for a cherry cupboard, $50 for a pine cottage bureau, up to $250 for a walnut or cherry chest of drawers. A running grandfather's clock can be found for $200, but a good cherry or walnut desk will run up to $500. Poster beds cost from $25 to $150, tester beds more. A finished dry sink will run about $60 to $100, a pine lift-top washstand about $45, a Windsor settee, $200. These prices are for finished pieces and taken at random from the ads while I write. But compare them with prices for new furniture of a good grade and you'll be surprised at the slight difference if any. Added to this, your antiques will increase in value while everyone knows the resale value of new furniture is very low.

I am often asked about mixing woods and periods. As to woods, I really don't think it matters as long as you keep the character of the furniture in line. By that I mean you wouldn't put crude pine primitives in the same room with a handsome mahogany highboy. But there is no reason why a maple table could not be used with a cherry cupboard. In the early days of cabinetmaking several kinds of wood might be combined in one piece. They used what they had and often stained them to match or painted the piece. Thus when an old secretary belonging to my grandfather was cleaned and re-finished we found it had a walnut frame, cherry-faced drawers, and a pine top. Periods can also be mixed with discretion. It costs money to be a perfectionist in this matter. But go easy on mixing Victorian with country pieces. They never seem to be compatible.

Don't overcrowd your antiques. Feature a fine piece and keep things simple. The overenthusiastic buyer can soon find herself swamped with too much stuff, until her house resembles a shop or a museum. I believe this is one reason why so many men are still "agin" antiques in the home. They hate the cluttered look. They have a horror of sitting on skimpy, wobbly chairs, of yanking at sticking drawers in old bureaus, or propping up the lid of a chest with loose hinges. Their idea of "antiques" is junk. But it doesn't have to be. Fortunately many men have become converts to antiques when they can be shown the economic worth of them. Men with workshops are having a wonderful time refinishing their own pieces. Men like good things. Show a man a beautifully finished old piece in perfect repair or an old clock that keeps perfect time, or a sturdy barroom chair that holds him comfortably, and he is ready to change his mind about antiques and often go the whole hog, outantiquing his wife if possible and usually ready to pay through the nose if he has to.

One of the finest things about a shared interest in antiques is that it gives a married couple something to do together. While the husband collects his guns and powder horns, mechanical banks, prints, or steins, the wife can indulge herself in china, glass, or other usable pieces for the home. They will take their antique excursions together and maybe even indulge in some good-natured rivalry. As one woman said to me, "Fred's bottle happy—I mean old, empty bottles. He had me drive fifty miles the other day on the trail of an Indian Princess bitters bottle. He got it for $12. I hope he's happy. Well, I'd rather be an 'antique' wife than a golf widow."

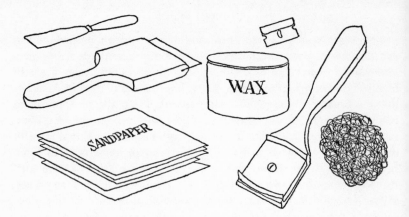

19. ROUGH OR FINISHED?

IF YOU have never refinished a piece of antique furniture you have never lived. It is an experience to be gone through once if never again. Because it will leave you—or the furniture—in one condition or another: with a half-finished piece and thorough disillusionment, or with something to crow about, a confirmed restorer who soon learns to talk glibly about the various merits of finishes, oils, stains, paint removers, and all the rest. In other words, restoring can be either fun if you take to it, or a terrible admission of failure. It depends more on one's degree of patience than upon skill, for doing over an old piece takes time, more time, and infinite pains.

There is, however, a decided advantage in buying furniture "in the rough." One of the things that ups the price of a good finished piece today is, of course, the cost of labor. Some dealers prefer to sell in the rough because they say they cannot make enough on the finished work. Some, who perhaps have their own workshop, do it themselves or have an old practiced hand to call on, prefer to sell the finished piece. Putting an old piece back into condition requires many hours of work, and if it has to be paid for at the rate of two or more dollars an hour you can see where it leaves you. It may explain some of the "quick tricks" you see in finished pieces, the planed table tops, the curious stains to hide new wood, the unrubbed-down varnishes, and so on.

There are several advantages in doing the work yourself. You can save money, you can have fun if you go about it the right way, and you can have the finish you like. There is a danger of over-finishing at the hands of a skilled worker; a "piano" finish is not for many old pieces. If it is old, you want it to look old, not battered but aged gracefully with years and usage. So you do it yourself. The main idea is not to hurry. Read the books. There are many good ones that tell you what to do, step by step. Buy good tools and the best supplies. It's worth it even if you do only one piece. You'll save the cost with your labor. Select for a first piece something easy, like a cottage chest of drawers. Chairs and tables are harder. Don't attempt to do over a fine piece until you have been graduated *summa cum laude* in the cabinetmaking school of experience.

The first step is either to preserve the old finish or strip it off. Unless a piece is terribly battered or mutilated or shows signs of having been badly redone at some time in its history, it may not even need refinishing. You'll be surprised at what a good washing with a mild soap and water will do. Adding three tablespoonfuls of boiled linseed oil and one tablespoonful of turpentine to a quart of the warm water helps to do a good cleaning job. Wash it off with clean water and when dry give it a good waxing. Don't try to put a new finish over an old one.

Suppose the piece has been painted. Are you going to strip it down to the wood or repaint? In the frantic effort to furnish whole rooms with "primitive" pine pieces that "go together" there has been a lot of taking down to the wood of furniture that was never intended to be that way. Most of the "fancy" chairs, the Windsors, side tables, Boston rockers, sinks, cupboards, etc., were painted originally and for a very good reason. They were not made of woods considered fine enough for good polished furniture and often because they were to be painted, they were made of several woods combined in one piece. So you see what happens when you take the paint off. Sometimes it may not matter that you have a pine cupboard with poplar doors or a chair with a hickory rung, but sometimes it does when the woods clash.

Let me tell you a story I just heard with a sad ending as I see it. A customer brought into my good friend and neighbor, Mr. C., who has done all my refinishing—and so beautifully!—a set of four Hitchcock chairs which had been in her family for three generations. They needed some repair and the old paint was worn. She wanted them taken down to the wood. Mr. C. did so under protest. What he found was not pine but poplar, not an attractive wood at best. So she decided to have them painted again. At her request Mr. C., who is not an artist, painted them black, striped them neatly in yellow, and *put decalcomanias on the back slats!* What she has now is practically nothing but four chairs to sit on. It would have been far better if she had had a new paint job done in the first place by an experienced decorator or had the old paint touched up. Terrible things have been done to old painted furniture by the amateur as well as by the artist with ability but no knowledge of the old painting skills. I am not an artist, but I know enough not to spoil an old piece. And once I did a good retouching job on my own. I redid a battered little washstand, the type with a hole for the bowl and holes and shelves for the other pieces. It had once been yellow, but not much was left except the old floral decoration on the top piece at the back. I looked through the books, found a formula for antique yellow, and painted it carefully, striped it in the original brown with a painter's striper, and then with an artist's oil-color brush I outlined around the old decoration most carefully with the yellow. Where the decoration was a bit rubbed I matched colors carefully and touched it up lightly and gently. The piece is a beauty today and still "original." I use it as a plant stand.

There are many fine books on decorating old furniture if you want to try it. You can get authentic stencil patterns and all kinds of gold and bronze paints and gold leaf. You can take lessons in freehand decorating from local teachers, at YWCAs, adult-education groups, etc. But please don't use decalcomanias. I know some very nice ones have been put out and I've used them for little things that do not require authentic decoration, old cans, boxes, etc. But for good old furniture, no!

When you consider that whole books have been written on doing over old furniture, what I tell you here will be but a drop in the bucket of information. But I would like to add a few hints from my own trial-and-error days and from watching my good angel, Mr. C., in his shop. I've taken off enough paint, it would seem, to cover

Grand Central Station and I've done it in a lot of ways. The best method is the use of any of the good commercial paint removers which get better every year. But sometimes you get hold of that tough old "buttermilk" paint that refuses to budge. If you use too much remover, it will often carry the paint into the pores of the soft wood. Then I go into scrapers. You have to be careful not to gouge the wood and you have to keep the scrapers sharp. You have to have them in many shapes—rounded, pointed, flat—to reach the various surfaces. You can also use glass if you wear gloves and throw the glass away when it gets dull. Penknives and razor blades help out in tight places. A sharp chisel and hammer will sometimes start a working point in hard paint.

One thing cannot be used, a torch for burning off the paint. It will scorch the wood even with care. Some people have had luck with the electric burner-scrapers. I can't seem to do very well with them. But I have learned to use an electric sander without taking off the patina. The belt kind that can move with the grain is best. But I have even developed a delicate touch with a rotary sander that leaves no deep marks that can't be taken off later by hand. Paint clogs the sanding disks, so they must be changed often. I've never tried a lye bath, the sure foe of old paint, but I've seen Mr. C. do it for stubborn pieces. It requires great care and a thorough scrubbing afterward to get the lye out of the wood, but it will get at that old red stain with which so many old pieces were finished. A washing with Clorox or oxalic acid, two ounces to one quart of water, will bleach it out, too, as well as remove other old deep-seated stains. Use household ammonia, one part to ten of water, to wash off either of these bleaches.

For finishing I prefer the shellac and wax treatment to the linseed oil. Linseed oil darkens wood and is a long, tedious process. It is also a dust-catcher. Pieces of soft wood, like pine or poplar, have to have some kind of filler, and shellac cut with half alcohol will do it. For very dry old wood Mr. C. feels it should be given a penetrating coat of oil first. Sometimes the shellac treatment will have to be repeated with a rubbing down with steel wool in between. If the patina has been left, it is better to use clear or white shellac. If the wood is too "raw," the darker brown shellac is better. But nothing hurts me more than to see an array of orangey pine pieces, the result of using orange shellac. There never was such wood; not even the old pumpkin pine could look that way.

While I would not recommend the method for fine pieces, I have finished off table tops that were going to take hard handling with a thinned-down coat of spar varnish for the filler, a second coat of pure spar varnish, and followed that with a coat of dull varnish. It gives the effect of wax, requires no care, and is not marred by water or alcohol. I do floors the same way.

For matching pieces I find it a good idea to stock up with several colors of oil stains—pine, maple, walnut, and mahogany. Then you can mix them to get what you want. Once I stained a new oak floor, made from second-grade wood I had bought cheap, to match the weathered pine paneling of the room, and it came out perfectly. I've even used shoe polish for getting a certain color. For filling holes and cracks you can color both plastic wood and putty with artists' oil colors. Stock up with burnt umber, burnt sienna, raw umber, raw sienna, yellow ochre, turkey red, and rose madder.

Never overlook the opportunity of buying up old wood, old floor boards of pine, poplar, perhaps even cherry, wall sidings of walnut and cherry or chestnut, broken-down furniture, wood from old barns and sheds, if you have the room to store it. I could go on and on. But you'll find your own tricks as you work, and you will get plenty of advice, good and bad. But again I say, read the books. And don't attempt to restore a valuable piece where a lot is at stake.

So much for furniture. What else can you do over? You can mend china and glass if they are not too badly broken. There are all sorts of cements and mending kits on the market if you want to get more professional. However, as with furniture, I'd prefer to let the professional handle the valuable piece. If you don't know where to find a good mender, ask your nearest antique dealer. But remember that no matter how cleverly mended, an imperfect piece will not bring the top price if you want to sell it. However, if it is rare or especially pleasing to you, it may pay to invest in having it repaired.

What do you do with dirty glass? Just plain soaking with soap and water and Clorox will often remove the sediment or ring from an old bottle or lamp font. Or let it soak for several days in a strong solution of washing soda or use household ammonia full strength. Sometimes shaking up a handful of BB gun shot or a piece of old chain in a glass piece will help to loosen the deposit. If all fails, you have probably got a piece of "sick" glass and not much can be done about it. To bleach age-browned china use Clorox.

Old silver needs an experienced hand. Wonders can be worked with it, dents taken out, hinges mended, new feet added, handles strengthened. If the piece is worth it, it is a good investment to save it. If you don't want to polish a badly tarnished piece of old metal, you can have it done by a professional burnisher and lacquered to keep it shining if you like it that way. You can have old nickel stripped from brass (many lamps, urns, etc. were nickelplated) and old silver from copper.

Leafing through the pages of the magazines that deal with antiques I am always impressed with the services that are advertised, things like rug mending, expert conditioning of old music boxes and other musical instruments, polishes of all kinds, knobs and drawer pulls, reproduction brasses for furniture, glass shades for lamps, frames for old pictures, quills for old inkwells, antique paints, doll wigs and parts, rattan, reed and rush for chair seats, among other things. In short, if you set out to have something fixed or want to do it yourself there is nothing to stop you—except, perhaps, a little money.

You can buy extenders for short beds (old ones are usually too short) and brackets to hold new box springs in old rope beds. Both things, however, can be managed very easily at home. The blacksmith or garageman will make you a set of heavy angle irons for screwing to the bed rails onto which you can *drop* the spring (otherwise the bed will be too high). You can have longer side rails made or you can piece the old ones. This, however, requires expert carpentry and much strengthening.

And while we are on the subject of beds, let me say one thing: you'll never find a pair of antique *twin* beds. If you want a pair of single beds, you'll have to go searching for two that are very close in style or have them altered to match. You won't always be able to get ready-made springs or mattresses for old beds because they were not uniform in size. Many were three-quarter beds. If it means a custom-made job, you'd better add that to the price you pay for the bed. There are firms which specialize in this work.

A word about lamps. A few years ago you had to take your old kerosene lamp or vase or what have you to an electrician to have it turned into an electric lamp. Today, it is a simple matter you can do yourself, for there are several big firms that specialize in everything pertaining to lamp conversion. Just read the ads. There are simple cork or expansion sockets to use with small-necked bottles, vases, or jugs. There are several sizes of screw-type sockets to fit almost any type of old kerosene burner. There are chimneys and glass shades of all kinds to replace the broken ones, some painted in the old manner, some expressly designed for student lamps and angle lamps. There are—and this is important—special electric bulbs to give realistic candle flames for sconces and chandeliers, some that can be used with a regular socket and some that require adapters. There is even a type of bulb that looks exactly like the flame of an old oil wick for lamps where not too much light is required. You can buy prisms, *bobêches*, reflectors, almost anything that will bring that old lamp or fixture back to life.

Don't fuss with the works of an old clock if you've never touched a clock since you tore down that old alarm clock as a kid. You can buy new hands, however, and new dials. You can have a reverse painting on glass done by an artist for an old door. You can pick up old weights and pendulums in some of the antique shops. But the works—better leave them alone. There are still many fine clockmakers who'll get the clock running for you.

Cane seating and rush seating can be learned, but they are tedious processes and not worth while unless you plan to use them often. Better give the work to someone else to take care of. The blind are very good at this work. In some places it is a project for the prisons.

For restoring paintings and books I suggest the professional unless you go into it for a hobby. You can clean up an old oil painting without much risk with soap and water with a little kerosene added to cut the grime. Do it gently, so as not to remove any paint, rinse and dry thoroughly before giving it a coat of artists' varnish. Gummed tape bought in the stationery shop will keep an old book from going to pieces, but if it is worth saving for posterity, put it in the proper hands.

I would never attempt to do anything with prints except perhaps clean off a border with art gum and then only if it is not torn. But prints can be cleaned and restored by professionals. Don't ever trim a print down to fit it in a frame. Prices of prints often depend upon size, and your scissors may be cutting off dollars.

20. REPRODUCTIONS AND FAKES

THERE is no doubt that the antique business is being threatened by the wave of dishonest reproductions being put on the market with the prime idea of deceiving the buyer. The dealers who have a living to make and prefer to do it the honest way are justly worried. One woman said to me the other day, "I am not going to buy any more glass. I'm afraid of it. The reproductions are too good. It is easy to be fooled." Another friend who has collected milk glass for years has practically stopped buying. "Unless I know positively where it has come from I'm afraid to touch it. There's too much bad stuff around, and it is not always easy to spot." Take cranberry glass. Without being warned, I noticed suddenly that there seemed to be a great quantity of it in the shops. It showed up at the antique shows. Why? I soon found out. It has been coming in from England, appealing, good-looking, but because of it good old American pieces have taken a dip in price.

Now all of this might tend to make the uninitiated in antiques afraid to go ahead and explore this fascinating subject. I would hate to think this is so. In spite of the stories, in spite of the books, there are still many fine and genuine things to be bought and enjoyed. Like the weather, you hear only the worst of it. But it does behoove one to be careful and not believe everything one sees and hears in the shops.

For those who have inherited their antiques, there is not much to fear. Of course a reproduction does not have to be recent. Chippendale and all the others were being copied a hundred years ago. But even such a copy would have a right to be called an antique. It is fairly safe to assume that a piece which has come down through two or more generations is genuine. On the other hand, if you are starting out to buy, you need to keep your fingers crossed.

This wave of wholesale reproductions seems to have struck the country about thirty years ago, when interest in antiques began to zoom. With prices rising in all directions, manufacturers saw a chance to cash in on them with pieces of cheap stuff close enough to the originals to fool the average buyer. Now right here it might be well to differentiate between a reproduction and a fake. A reproduction can be a fake or turn into a fake if it was made or sold to deceive the buyer. But it can also sell for just what is is. A fake, on the other hand, is always a reproduction and usually a very good one, aimed to be passed off as the real thing.

Beware of covered animal dishes of opaque white glass like this!

The big question is, who is to blame? Much of this reproduction stuff is made honestly and intended to be honestly distributed for those who cannot afford the real thing but have a feeling for the early American *décor*. Many companies put out reproductions just for this reason. Department stores, gift shops, and furniture shops are full of their wares. Their catalogues are fascinating. Some advertise that their glass or iron is being made over the old molds. It could well be. But along the line much can happen to turn these reproductions from honest merchandise into fakes.

Perhaps a canny jobber sees a chance to reap a good profit if he calls the reproductions old. He makes the rounds of the antique shops dropping a piece or two as he goes to dealers who may or may not know what they are buying. If he finds a crooked dealer, he may leave a case of them to be oozed into the stock, one by one. He may "salt" a sale with his fakes, hide them in out-of-the-way places to be "discovered" by the unwary buyer, in old barns, attics, or sheds, but in any case he is getting at least a dollar on every ten cents he has invested.

I well remember when old trivets began to be popular, about fifteen years ago. I used to attend a regular monthly sale run by an astute countryman turned antique dealer. At first his sales were exciting adventures. He had an "in" to the old houses for miles around. But his sales began to get so popular that he found himself unable to keep up with the demand. Then things began to happen. I had bought many an iron piece—forks, spoons, ladles, as well as old trivets—from him for as low as ten cents. But then the trivet business boomed. Trivets were going good for $1. He seemed to have a lot of them. I got suspicious. Poking around in the back of the fire hall where perhaps I should not have been I found cartons of them, all new. I never trusted that man again. I never went to any more of his sales. A month or two later I saw the ad in a magazine for these same trivets "made over the old molds." Henry had found them first and cashed in before the knowledge got around. Henry also began to sell a lot of ruby overlay lamps with marble bases. He was always careful not to call them antique. He merely held them up and let the buyer beware. There were plenty who bought them believing them old.

Of course the terrible thing about such practices is that so often these fakes reach the honest dealer by a roundabout route and are accepted as originals in all good faith. They will continue to circulate for many years, until no one will know what is real and what is not. Not much can be done about it, except by educating the public and exposing the fakes as they appear. Steps are being urged to make such deception illegal and deserving of punishment.

It has been said that there are only a handful of real experts in the country who can be trusted to sift out the good from the spurious. This does not mean that all fakes cannot be easily spotted. They can, especially in the cheaper brackets. But for the terribly expensive and rare pieces there are experts on the other side of the fence, too, who know all the identification points the authorities are going to look for and they are able to keep a step ahead. Worm holes, dust, wear and tear of time, stains, labels, patina, all can be imitated. There are workmen who can turn out as fine joining and turning and carving by hand as on the original from which they copy. Even the problem of old wood is surmounted by using wood from old pieces too far gone for wholesale restoration or reproduction. Or for elaborating, carving, etc., on plain pieces to bring them up to a certain period or value. This is called "glorification."

The Hitchcock painted chair is still being made today.

I have often heard people say with some amusement, "Well, after all, what does it matter? If it looks exactly the same as the old piece and nobody knows that it isn't, what difference does it make? You can enjoy it just the same." True, there are some "ostrich" buyers who don't *want* to know if they have an ersatz piece. They can still point with pride—and pride has a lot to do with owning antiques—to the rare English lantern clock or the Philadelphia highboy they have acquired, letting the responsibility of its authenticity rest on the person they have bought it from. But if money means anything, they must admit they have paid through the nose for something worth probably only a tenth of the price. This counts when it is a period piece worth more than a thousand dollars. It is not too bad when you pay $10 for a goblet worth probably fifty cents. It also means that if you should have to sell, or your estate has to sell your holdings, you will lose money on these bogus pieces when the appraisers get busy.

So all this being true, what can you do about it? First of all, know your stuff. Study and examine before you set out to buy. You may make mistakes at first, but soon you'll begin to get the "feel" of old things. Your fingertips will catch the too-dull edges of a pontil mark that has been impressed on new glass where no mark from a broken-off pontil ever existed; you'll feel the undulating surfaces made by old tools, you'll recognize discrepancies in height and weight, the off-color of a colored piece, the new turning of a screw, the "glare" of new wood against the patina of old. You'll learn to look for wear on an old chair leg that has been dragged over a floor for years, wear on the runners of old drawers, shrinkage of round table tops, pitting of old pewter and iron, and sharper patterns in old pressed glass. You may even learn to smell old wood—experts say they can. With familiarity and much handling you develop an intuition, a sixth sense, and become able to spot wrong glass lids on dishes and wrong stoppers on cruets and decanters. You'll learn that mended china will show up under violet ray. Such detecting is a lot of fun if nothing else. The idea is, if you have doubts, don't hurry. And the more important the piece, the more investigation and study you should give it.

You should try to find out where the piece you want to buy came from. You won't always be too successful about this. Even an honest dealer may hesitate to tell for various reasons. But often you will get a straight answer that you can follow up if you want to do so. Perhaps the most important thing is to know your dealer.

Now this is a difficult problem—to know whether a dealer is honest or not. I asked a friend of mine who has just gone into the antique business, and whose character is beyond reproach, how one can tell. She could give me no hard-and-fast rules. Probably the first consideration is the personal integrity of the shop owner. If he is well spoken of in other directions, if neighbors think well of him, if he has satisfied customers, if he admits his doubts or ignorance, has been known to take back things which have been proved not to be what he represented, if his business dealings in his town or community are good, his bank credit sound, his contacts with other dealers friendly, if he has been in business at the same location for some time, you can feel fairly sure of him. Those who make "mistakes" are soon smoked out and have to move on. It is the fly-by-night boys whom you have to distrust. A dishonest trader cannot operate long without something coming out about his dealings. Be careful, however, of plain malicious gossip. Jealousy may dictate it or customers dissatisfied for some other reason. A "sharp" dealer is not necessarily a dishonest one. He may merely be too canny to be pleasant.

You will say, "That's all very well, but how am I going to find out all that when I go into a strange shop for the first time and see a Currier and Ives print I've always wanted? Maybe it's old and maybe it isn't. Maybe the dealer is a crook, for all I know."

True, you can't go into credentials for one small purchase. You will just have to use your head and take your chance. Sometimes the very "feel" of the shop gives it away, sometimes the price. If you know what you ought to pay for that print and you find it quite a bit cheaper, a "bargain," you begin to wonder why. No one has to cut a price on a *wanted* piece. But the dishonest dealer figures you are not going to be too fussy about going into details if you are getting a bargain. If you find too much of something supposedly rare, stop and think. A young couple I knew who were touring New England saw some ruby goblets they coveted. But money was low, and so they passed them up. A few miles farther down the line they went into another shop and saw the same goblets. By the time they'd seen them in a third shop they were very glad they'd thought twice at the first one.

On the whole, I would advise anyone making a big and important purchase to make it close to home, where you can do some investigation before you buy. I would suggest you look for specialists in the field, a dealer who goes in heavily for one thing, like Oriental Lowestoft (Chinese Import China) or Wedgwood, or pine primitives. Again I say shop around and ask questions. Once you have made contact with a thoroughly honest dealer whom you trust you may often have to go no further. When he knows your wants, he'll do the looking for you. An honest dealer will also not hesitate to give you a guarantee with your purchase if it is important enough and agree to take it back if you find it not what has been represented. He wants no stigma of crooked dealing attached to his name. I've noticed recently in some ads that the dealers "guarantee" their stuff to be old.

If you see yourself launched on a program of antique buying, it would certainly pay you to read the books and articles in the maga-

zines which are exposing fake reproductions and telling you how to
spot them. Such articles are invaluable to the whole antique business.
More of them will be welcomed. I know of no complete listing of
fakes—the subject is too broad a one to be covered that way and the
picture is constantly changing. Once the cat is out of the bag, the
fake loses prestige and may end up in the five-and-ten. But various
authorities in the field are always on the alert. Follow their findings.

So don't be afraid, just be cautious. Learn all you can about the
particular thing you are interested in. Cultivate the dealers. There
is still plenty of good stuff around to be bought and enjoyed.

Suggestions for Beginning Collectors

What makes a collector? Accident, very often. A few inherited
pieces, an unusual gift of an antique, a casual purchase, and you
are off on a new and exciting hobby. The main requirement for a
good collector is the insatiable curiosity of a true detective, perhaps
also a touch of magpie acquisitiveness. Certainly collecting anything
makes a fine escape pastime, but the more significant the thing collected the better when and if it comes to selling off the collection
later on. When it comes to antiques, there are many, many things
of interest that are not in the high-price bracket and not hard to
find for the beginning collector. A fine way to start is to select
something akin to your work or profession. Aside from many things
suggested in the various chapters I have made a list of collectibles
which ought to open up many avenues of interest:

Farmers' Cups	Birdcages
Apothecary Jars	Horse Brasses
Apothecary Bottles	Bridle Rosettes
Tobacco Jars	Marbles
Tobacco Boxes	Chess Figures
Bookmarks	Character Bottles
Eagles	Napkin Rings
Madonnas	Match Safes
Holy-water Fonts	Salt Dips
Pipe Stoppers	Ship Models
Candy Molds	Historical Handkerchiefs
Cookie Cutters	Powder Boxes

Fairy Lamps
Playing Cards
Glass, China, and Metal Slippers
Glass, China, and Metal Shoes
Glass, China, and Metal Hats
Drawing Books
Mustache Cups
Pocket Match Safes
Pipes
Squeak Toys
Cruets
Candy Jars
Pottery Figures
Sleight-of-hand Pieces
Theater Programs
Kate Greenaway Items
Mirror Knobs
Tiebacks
Any Animal Figure
Victorian Hands
Music Boxes
Sheet Music
Spoons (Apostle, Monkey, Love, etc.)
Souvenir Spoons
Canes
Thimbles
Pincushions
Card Cases

Tiles
Decoy Ducks
Barber Bottles
Souvenir Red-and-white Glass
Toy Candy Containers
Inkwells
Butter Chips
Shaving-soap Boxes
Easter Eggs
Figures of Fictional Characters
Pretzel Antiques
Tobies
Perfume Bottles
Whistles
Postcards
Doorknobs
Bookplates
Tools
Hourglasses
Tea Cozies
Sewing Birds
Auto License Plates
Paper Cutters
Cuspidors
Flags
Timetables
Zodiac Emblems

The Things You Hear

Following is a list of one hundred terms more or less familiar to the expert but needing definition if you don't speak antiquese:

Air Twist—Said of the stems of wineglasses which have a swirled effect.

Angelica Kauffman—Swiss portrait painter of the eighteenth century who set the style for much furniture and china embellishment.

Apron—Any flat facing piece of wood that drops from a seat or other edge.

Bag Sewing Table—Usually Sheraton in style with gathered silk sewing bag well under the drawer or drawers.

Bar Lip—Heavy mouth edge of a bottle or flask made by rolling back the glass for extra thickness.

Basalt—Black china paste developed by Wedgwood and made by others of his time.

Beaker—Small drinking vessel with flared top, no handles.

Bible Box—Early box of carved wood, usually oak with sloping hinged top for keeping family Bible.

Birdcage Table—Tilt-top with square spindled cage on top of pedestal—usually tip-and-turn Chippendale type.

Bitters—Highly alcoholic vegetable potion sold "for the health" in bitters bottles of the nineteenth century.

Bob—Adjustable weight on a clock pendulum.

Bonnet Top—Said of a highboy or secretary or clock when the top line is broken and features a central unit.

Bosom Bottle—Small bottle used as a perfume holder and worn in the bosom.

Bracket Foot—Right-angle support on the corner of a piece of furniture, often scrolled or ogee molded.

Breadboard Ends—Flush end boards of a table or door running crosswise to the main boards to prevent warping and to hide the rough sawed edges.

Bridle Rosette—Small fancy button of glass or metal for decorating a horse's bridle.

Bull's-eye Glass—Pane of glass in which a swirled glob of glass was left in the center in the making.

Calabash Bottle—Gourd-shaped bottle or flask.

Caudle Cup—Two-handled drinking mug of the seventeenth and eighteenth centuries, often with a lid.

Chamfered—Beveling on the sharp edges of furniture.

Circa—Handy word used to approximate a date.

Clock Jack—Wind-up instrument with springs for turning a spit over an open fire.

Coffin Cupboard—Cupboard with paneled doors, the panels shaped like coffins.

Commode—A side table; also a washstand.

Cotton Spiral—Opaque white spiraling in the stem of a blown wineglass.

Courting Mirror—Small mirror with pieces of mirror set in the wooden frame as decoration. Often Chinese.

Deal—Another name for pine.

Dentil—Term meaning notched or serrated. Said of moldings or carved decoration.

Distaff—That part of a spinning wheel that holds the raw wool or flax.

Distelfink—Pennsylvania Dutch word for a finchlike bird often seen in their peasant decorations.

Dowel—Round wooden pin used in place of nails or screws.

Dr. Syntax Plates—With pictures after the Rowlandson illustrations published in 1812.

Draw Table—Extension table enlarged by drawing out sections from underneath the top.

Epergne—Table centerpiece with various tiered units for holding flowers, fruit, etc.

Finial—Decorative top piece of a clock, secretary, chair back, etc. Or knob on a china or glass lid.

Fireboard—Wooden screen that fits the opening of a fireplace when not in use. Often decorated.

Fire Bucket—Leather bucket used in olden days to carry water for fire fighting. Often decorated with insignia of the fire company that owned it.

Flip Glass—Large drinking glass for flip which was mixed by tossing from one glass to another. Made from beer, brandy, eggs, lemon peel, and spices, and heated with a hot poker.

Frow—Splitting tool for making shingles.

Frozen Charlotte—One-piece china doll with no movable parts.

Gallery—Shallow raised edge on sides of tray or table top.

Gemel—Double bottle.

Girandole—Branched candle holder or the bracket on a mirror frame. Also the round convex mirror of about 1800.

Gophering Iron—Fluted iron of various types for ironing ruffles.

Haircloth—Stiff woven cloth using horse's hair.

Hallmark—Maker's mark on silver.

Harvest Ring—Jug in the shape of a ring for hanging over the arm to carry liquids to men in the fields.

Jasper Ware—Hard, unglazed stoneware having relief designs in white or contrasting color. Made by Wedgwood and others.

Joiner—A cabinetmaker.

Kettle Front—Any furniture piece with a bowed or bulging front.

Knife Boxes—Deep, slope-topped boxes of fine wood for the ends of a sideboard for holding silver.

Knife Rest—Small table piece usually of glass for keeping the carving knife off the cloth between usings.

Lazy Boy—Pipe tongs with scissorslike handles which extend or shorten by means of a series of toggle joints.

Linenfold—A kind of carving for panels resembling the vertical folds of linen.

Latticinio—Latticelike network of glass threads within clear glass.

Lavabo—Wall reservoir and basin for holding water for washing hands. Pewter, silver, china, tin, etc.

Millefiori—"Thousand flowers." Glass canes cut to give appearance of many small flowers within clear glass of paperweights, marbles, etc.

Mule Chest—Tall blanket chest that looks like four-drawered bureau but upper part is chest with two top drawers only simulated.

Muntins—Wooden moldings that separate panes of glass in doors, windows, etc.

Nailsea—English fancy glass of opaque white decorated with colored swirls, loops, etc.

Nodder—Ornament or toy with balanced head that keeps nodding at the touch of a finger.

OG—Double-curved, S-type molding or bracket.

Papier-mâché—Material made from paper pulp and resin pressed and hardened. Painted to resemble fine lacquer work.

Patina—Natural surface of old wood or metal. Sign of age.

Piggin—Staved bucket with one stave extending for a handle.

Plinth—Square part or base of a column.

Pontil Mark—Rough spot on the bottom of a piece of glass where the object was snapped off from the glassmaker's rod. Sign of a blown piece. Often smoothed off.

Poonah—Stenciling on velvet.

Porringer—Small shallow dish with one or two flat handles. No cover.

Pounce—Black sand for use in desk sander.

Pricket Stick—Candlestick with a spike for the candle instead of a socket.

Primitive—Word used for antiques made by untrained craftsmen; or early forms of certain pieces, particularly the cruder "country" items.

Pristine—Original state or condition, not altered.

Proof—Without flaws. Also *Mint*.

Pumpkin Pine—Variety of deep orangey pine found in many primitive pieces.

Pung Seat—Removable wagon seat.

Puzzle Mug—Trick mug with several spouts or openings which douses the unwary drinker. Trick is to cover all but one with the fingers.

Rabbeted—Said of joints where one piece is cut away to take another piece made to fit into it.

Raked—The angle at which the legs of a chair or table extend when slanted.

Rattail—Describes the thin, curved end of a wrought-iron piece. Also the handle of a silver spoon where it meets the bowl.

Reeding—Parallel lines of beading for furniture decoration.

Saddle Seat—Heavy wooden chair seat shaped like a saddle to accommodate body contour more comfortably.

Sander—Shaker used with inkwell to sprinkle sand over wet ink in place of more modern blotter.

Slip Seat—Removable chair seat, usually upholstered.

Splayed—Slanted or turning outward. Said of legs of a table or chair.

Standish—Desk set consisting of inkwell, sander, quill holder, or wafer box.

Stretchers—Supporting crosspieces which connect the legs of a table or chair.

Sulphides—Type of paperweight or marble where a silvery figure is encased in the clear glass. Figure made of white clay.

Tambour—Flexible sliding door or panel on furniture made by gluing slats of wood on heavy cloth.

Tappit Hen—Metal measure with rounded body, thin neck, and flared mouth and lid.

Theorem—Stenciled picture.

Till—Small drawer or section within a chest usually with its own lid. Often concealed for money.

Tin Kitchen—Reflector oven for use beside an open fire.

Toile—French printed chintz. Indian and other Oriental patterns.

Tole—French word for old tin, especially when painted.

Touch Mark—Mark of the pewterer.

Trencher—Deep wooden plate.

Wagon Seat—A wide, deep seat usually with curved spindled back.

Wainscot Chair—Heavy chair with a high, straight back, carved or paneled.

Witch Ball—Large ball of blown colored glass to hang in the window to keep away the witches.

Museums and Restorations

There is no better way to familiarize yourself with antiques than to visit the museum in your locality, or those nearby when you are traveling, where collections of Americana are featured. And don't miss the big restorations as you roll along the highway on your vacation. Listed below are a few of the outstanding places to visit, but it scarcely scratches the surface of all the collections and houses throughout the country devoted to American antiques. I would suggest that you use the *AAA Tour Books* of the American Automobile Association for further listings of interesting houses and museums. There are three of these, Northeastern, Southeastern, and Western, covering the whole country, and they miss practically nothing of historic and antique interest. They can be obtained at any AAA office—free to members.

Museums

Metropolitan Museum of Art, New York City (American Wing)
Museum of the City of New York
New York Historical Society
Cooper Union Museum for the Arts of Decoration, New York City
Brooklyn Museum
Museum of Clocks and Watches of the New York University, Bronx, New York
Home Insurance Co. Museum, New York City
Corning Glass Museum, Corning, New York
The Farm Museum, Cooperstown, New York
Philadelphia Museum of Art, Philadelphia, Pennsylvania
Atwater Kent Museum, Philadelphia, Pennsylvania
Washington Memorial Museum, Valley Forge, Pennsylvania
Museum of the Chester County Historical Society, West Chester, Pennsylvania

Museum of the Bucks County Historical Society, Doylestown. Pennsylvania

Pennsylvania Historical Society, Philadelphia, Pennsylvania

Berks County Historical Society Museum, Reading, Pennsylvania

Pennsylvania Farm Museum, Landis Valley, Lancaster County, Pennsylvania

Hershey Museum, Hershey, Pennsylvania

Moravian Historical Society, Nazareth, Pennsylvania

Schwenkfelder Library, Pennsburg, Pennsylvania

Henry Francis du Pont Winterthur Museum, Winterthur, Delaware

Valentine Museum, Richmond, Virginia

Lightner Museum, St. Augustine, Florida

Cincinnati Art Museum, Cincinnati, Ohio

Art Institute of Chicago, Illinois

Henry Ford Collection, Dearborn, Michigan

Detroit Museum of Fine Arts, Detroit, Michigan

William Rockhill Nelson Museum, Kansas City, Missouri

Shelburne Museum, Shelburne, Vermont

Bennington Museum, Bennington, Vermont

Essex Institute, Salem, Massachusetts

Wells Museum, Southboro, Massachusetts

Museum of Fine Arts, Boston, Massachusetts

Rhode Island School of Design, Providence, Rhode Island

Hartford Atheneum, Hartford, Connecticut

Gallery of Fine Arts, Yale University, New Haven, Connecticut

Toy Museum, Old Lyme, Connecticut

Albert Pike Museum, Winslow, Arkansas

Historical Society Museum, Wilmington, Delaware

Children's Museum, Nashville, Tennessee

Washington State Historical Society Museum, Tacoma, Washington

Dallas Museum, Dallas, Texas

Seattle Historical Museum, Washington

Union Pacific Museum of History, Omaha, Nebraska

St. Joseph's Museum, St. Joseph, Missouri

Folk Art Museum, Santa Fe, New Mexico

Houses and Restorations

Williamsburg, Virginia
The Cloisters, Ephrata, Pennsylvania
1704 House, West Chester, Pennsylvania
Washington's Headquarters, Valley Forge, Pennsylvania
Fairmont Park Houses, Philadelphia, Pennsylvania
Pennsbury (Wm. Penn House), Tullytown, Pennsylvania
Hopewell Village, Birdsboro, Pennsylvania
Old Sturbridge Village, Sturbridge, Massachusetts
Deerfield Village, Deerfield, Massachusetts
Greenfield Village, Dearborn, Michigan
Open House Days, Newcastle, Delaware
Open House Days, Natchez, Mississippi
Open House Days, Wiscasset, Maine
Monticello, Charlottesville, Virginia
Mt. Vernon, Virginia
Maryland House and Garden Pilgrimage (April-May)
Old Salem Restoration, Winston-Salem, North Carolina
Old Houses, Galena, Illinois
Black House, Ellsworth, Maine
Sunnyside Restoration, Irvington-on-the-Hudson, New York
Old Irelandville Restoration, Watkins Glen, New York
Philipse Manor, Tarrytown, New York
Jamestown Restoration, Virginia
Van Courtlandt House, New York City
Dyckman House, New York City
Jumel Mansion, New York City
Carlyle House, Alexandria, Virginia
Stratford Hall, Stratford, Virginia
Paul Revere House, Boston, Massachusetts
The Old Manse, Concord, Massachusetts
John Brown House, Providence, Rhode Island
Whitehall, Middletown, Rhode Island
Mission Inn, Riverside, California
Afton Villa, St. Francisville, Louisiana
Falsington Village Restoration, Falsington, Pennsylvania

Bibliography

CHAPTER 1

BOWLES, ELLA S. *About Antiques*. Philadelphia: J. B. Lippincott Co., 1929.

DREPPERD, CARL. *First Reader for Antique Collectors*. New York: Doubleday & Company, Inc.

——. *Victorian, the Cinderella of Antiques*. New York: Doubleday & Company, Inc.

ORMSBEE, THOMAS. *Collecting Antiques in America*. New York: Robert M. McBride Co., Inc., 1940.

WINCHESTER, ALICE. *How to Know American Antiques*. New York: New American Library.

CHAPTER 3

Antiques Price Guide. Uniontown, Pennsylvania: E. G. Warman Publishing Co.

Bottle Price Guide. Uniontown, Pennsylvania: E. G. Warman Publishing Co.

JACOBS, CARL. *A Price Guide to American Pewter*. Southwick, Massachusetts: Privately printed.

LAIDACKER, SAMUEL. *Anglo-American China*. 2 vols. Bristol, Pennsylvania: Privately printed.

LEE, RUTH WEBB. *Current Values of Antique Glass*. Framingham Centre, Massachusetts: Privately printed.

——. *Price Guide to Pattern Glass*. Framingham Centre, Massachusetts: Privately printed.

Milk Glass Price Guide. Uniontown, Pennsylvania: E. G. Warman Publishing Co.

ORMSBEE, THOMAS. *Prime Antiques and Their Current Prices*. New York: Robert M. McBride Co., Inc., 1947.

Print Price Guide. Uniontown, Pennsylvania: E. G. Warman Publishing Co.

The Second Goblet Price Guide. Uniontown, Pennsylvania: E. G. Warman Publishing Co.

WARE, W. PORTER. *Occupational Shaving Mugs and Their Prices*. Chicago: Lightner Publishing Company.

CHAPTER 4

CHAMBERLAIN, NARCISSA. *Old Rooms for New Living.* New York: Hastings House Publishers, Inc., 1953.

FREEMAN, LARRY. *How to Price Antiques.* Watkins Glen, New York: Century House.

ORMSTON, FRANK. *Antiques for Profit.* New York: Greenberg: Publisher.

ROLLINS, ALICE R. *Antiques for the Home.* New York: Harper & Brothers, 1926.

Washer's Directory of Antique Dealers. San Francisco: Privately printed.

WINCHESTER, ALICE. *Living with Antiques.* New York: Robert M. McBride Co., Inc., 1914, 1922; Dodd, Mead & Co., 1941.

CHAPTER 5

ANDREWS, E. D., and ANDREWS, F. *Shaker Furniture.* New Haven: Yale University Press, 1937, 1950.

ARONSON, JOSEPH. *Encyclopedia of Furniture.* New York: Crown Publishers, Inc.

BURROUGHS, P. H. *Southern Antiques.* Richmond, Virginia: Garrett & Massie, Inc., 1931.

DOWNS, JOSEPH. *American Furniture.* New York: The Macmillan Co.

DREPPERD, CARL. *Handbook of Antique Chairs.* New York: Doubleday & Company, Inc.

FREEMAN, LARRY. *Federal and Empire Furniture.* Watkins Glen, New York: Century House.

LAZEARE, JAMES. *Primitive Pine Furniture.* Watkins Glen, New York: Century House.

MILLER, EDGAR, JR. *American Antique Furniture.* New York: M. Barrows & Co., Inc., 1948; Greystone Press, 1950.

NUTTING, WALLACE. *Furniture Treasury.* 3 vols. New York: The Macmillan Co.

ORMSBEE, THOMAS. *Field Guide to American Victorian Furniture.* Boston: Little, Brown & Co., 1952.

———. *Field Guide to Early American Furniture.* Boston: Little, Brown & Co., 1951.

ROBACKER, EARL F. *Pennsylvania Dutch Stuff.* Philadelphia: University of Pennsylvania Press, 1944.

SACK, ALBERT. *Fine Points of Furniture.* New York: Crown Publishers, Inc.

CHAPTER 6

BELKNAP, E. M. *Milk Glass*. New York: Crown Publishers, Inc.

BERGSTROM, EVANGELINE H. *Old Glass Paperweights*. Chicago: Lakeside Press.

DANIELS, DOROTHY. *Cut and Engraved Glass (1771-1905)*. New York: M. Barrows & Co., Inc.

FREEMAN, LARRY. *Iridescent Glass*. Watkins Glen, New York: Century House.

JOKELSON, PAUL. *Antique French Paperweights*. New York: Micomex, Inc.

KAMM, MINNIE WATSON. *Pitcher Books*. 8 vols. Watkins Glen, New York: Century House.

LEE, RUTH WEBB. *Early American Pressed Glass*. Framingham Centre, Massachusetts: Privately printed.

———. *Handbook of Early American Glass Patterns*. Framingham Centre, Massachusetts: Privately printed.

———. *Nineteenth-Century Art Glass*. Framingham Centre, Massachusetts: Privately printed.

———. *Sandwich Glass*. Framingham Centre, Massachusetts: Privately printed.

———. *Victorian Glass*. Framingham Centre, Massachusetts: Privately printed.

MAUST, DON. *Bottle and Glass Handbook*. Uniontown, Pennsylvania: E. G. Warman Publishing Company.

MCKEARIN, HELEN, and GEORGE S. *American Glass*. New York: Crown Publishers, Inc.

MILLARD, DR. S. T. *Goblets*. Topeka, Kansas: Kansas Central Press, 1938.

WATKINS, LAURA. *Cambridge Glass*. Boston: Little, Brown & Co., 1930.

CHAPTER 7

BAKER, W. D. JOHN, and WARREN. *Old English Lustre Pottery*.

BARBER, EDWIN ATLEE. *Pottery and Porcelain of the United States*. New York: G. P. Putnam's Sons.

CAMEHL, ADA WALKER. *The Blue China Book*. New York: Tudor Publishing Co.

EARLE, ALICE M. *China Collecting in America*. New York: Charles Scribner's Sons, 1892; Empire State Book Company, 1924.

EYLES, DESMOND. *Good Sir Toby*. London: Doulton & Co., Ltd.

FREEMAN, LARRY. *Majolica*. Watkins Glen, New York: Century House.

HAGGAR, REGINALD. *Staffordshire Chimney Ornaments*. New York: Pitman Publishing Corporation.

HUGHES, BERNARD, and THERLE. *English China and Bone Porcelain*. London: Lutterworth Press.

KAMM, MINNIE WATSON. *Old China*. Watkins Glen, New York: Century House.

LAIDACKER, SAMUEL. *Anglo-American China*. 2 vols. Bristol, Pennsylvania: Privately printed.

LICHTEN, FRANCES. *Folk Art of Rural Pennsylvania*. New York: Charles Scribner's Sons, 1946.

McCLINTON, KATHARINE MORRISON. *A Handbook of Popular Antiques*. New York: Random House.

RAMSAY, JOHN. *American Potters and Pottery*. Boston: Hale, Cushman & Flint, 1938.

SCHLEIGER, ARLENE. *200 Patterns of Haviland China*. Omaha, Nebraska: Privately printed.

SPARGO, JOHN. *Early American Pottery and China*. Watkins Glen, New York: Century House, 1926.

THORN, C. JORDAN. *Handbook of Old Pottery and Porcelain Marks*. New York: Tudor Publishing Co.

CHAPTER 8

BRADBURY, FREDERICK. *A History of Old Sheffield Plate*. London: The Macmillan Co., 1912.

BUHLER, KATHRYN C. *American Silver*. Cleveland: The World Publishing Company.

BURGESS, FRED W. *Silver, Pewter, and Sheffield Plate*. London: Routledge & Kegan Paul Ltd., 1921.

ENSKO, STEPHEN G. C. *American Silversmiths and Their Marks*. New York: Robert Ensko, Inc., 1948.

FREEMAN, LARRY, and BEAUMONT, JANE. *American Plated Silver*. Watkins Glen, New York: Century House.

KERFOOT, J. B. *American Pewter*. Boston: Houghton Mifflin Co., 1924.

LAUGHLIN, LESLIE I. *Pewter in America*. Boston: Houghton Mifflin Co., 1940.

STUTZENBERGER, ALBERT. *The American Story in Spoons*. Louisville, Kentucky: Privately printed.

THORN, C. JORDAN. *Handbook of American Silver and Pewter Marks*. New York: Tudor Publishing Co.

WYLER, S. B. *The Book of Sheffield Plate*. New York: Crown Publishers, Inc.

CHAPTER 9

BURGESS, F. W. *Chats on Old Copper and Brass.* New York: A. A. Wyn, Inc., 1955.

COLEMAN, S. N. *Book of Bells.* New York: The John Day Co., 1938.

GATTY, MARGARET. *Book of Sundials.* London: Bell & Sons, Ltd., 1900.

LINDSAY, J. S. *Iron and Brass Implements of English and American Homes.* Boston: Medici Society.

MCCLINTON, KATHARINE MORRISON. *Antique Collecting.* Greenwich, Connecticut: Fawcett Publications, Inc.

MOORE, N. HUDSON. *Old Pewter, Brass, Copper, and Sheffield Plate.* Philadelphia: Frederick A. Stokes Company, 1905.

NORTHEND, M. N. *Historical Doorways of Old Salem.* Boston: Houghton Mifflin Co., 1926.

ORMSBEE, THOMAS H. *Care and Repair of Antiques.* New York: Robert M. McBride Co., Inc., 1949.

SPRINGER, LOIS. "Jingle Bell Town," *Hobbies* (December, 1956).

CHAPTER 10

BULAU, ALWIN E. *Footprints of Assurance.* New York: The Macmillan Co.

CHRISTENSEN, EDWIN. *Index of American Design.* New York: The Macmillan Co., 1950.

DREPPERD, CARL. *Victorian, the Cinderella of Antiques.* New York: Doubleday & Company, Inc.

LINDSAY, J. S. *Iron and Brass Implements of English and American Homes.* Boston: Medici Society.

LIPMAN, JEAN. *American Folk Decoration.* New York: Oxford University Press, Inc.

MCCLINTON, KATHARINE MORRISON. *Antique Collecting.* Greenwich, Connecticut: Fawcett Publications, Inc.

MERCER, HENRY C. *The Bible in Iron.* Doylestown, Pennsylvania: Bucks County Historical Society.

SONN, ALBERT H. *Early American Wrought Iron.* 2 vols. New York: Charles Scribner's Sons, 1928.

CHAPTER 11

CHRISTENSEN, EDWIN. *Index of American Design.* New York: The Macmillan Co., 1950.

DREPPERD, CARL. *Pioneer America.* New York: Doubleday & Company, Inc.

GOULD, MARY EARLE. *Early American Woodenware.* Springfield, Massachusetts: The Pond-Ekberg Company, 1942.

HALL, PEG. *Early American Decorating Patterns*. New York: M. Barrows & Co., Inc., 1951.

LICHTEN, FRANCES. *Folk Art of Rural Pennsylvania*. New York: Charles Scribner's Sons, 1946.

McCLINTON, KATHARINE MORRISON. *Antique Collecting*. Greenwich, Connecticut: Fawcett Publications, Inc.

MURRAY, MARIA D. *The Art of Tray Painting*. New York: Studio Publications, Inc.

RAMSAY, JOHN. *American Potters and Pottery*. Boston: Hale, Cushman & Flint, 1938.

RICE, A. H., and STOUDT, JOHN BAER. *Shenandoah Pottery*. Strasburg, Virginia: Halley Publishing Co.

CHAPTER 12

BRITTEN, F. J. *Old Clocks and Watches*. London: R. T. Batsford, Ltd., 1922.

MOORE, N. HUDSON. *The Old Clock Book*. New York: Tudor Publishing Co., 1936.

NUTTING, WALLACE. *The Clock Book*. Framingham Centre, Massachusetts: Privately printed, 1924.

PALMER, BROOKS. *Book of American Clocks*. New York: The Macmillan Co.

SPEAR, DOROTHEA E. *American Watch Papers*. Worcester, Massachusetts: American Antiquarian Society.

CHAPTER 13

DREPPERD, CARL. *First Reader for Antique Collectors*. New York: Doubleday & Company, Inc.

FREEMAN, LARRY. *Lights on Old Lamps*. Watkins Glen, New York: Century House.

HAYWARD, ARTHUR. *Colonial Lighting*. Boston: B. J. Brimmer Co., 1923.

McKEARIN, GEORGE S., and HELEN. *American Glass*. New York: Crown Publishers, Inc.

TIBBETTS, DOROTHY. *Clarke's Fairy Lamps*. Worcester, Massachusetts: American Antiquarian Society, 1952.

CHAPTER 14

BURGESS, FRED W. *Old Prints and Engravings*. New York: Tudor Publishing Co., 1937.

CARRICK, ALICE VAN LEER. *Shades of Our Ancestors*. Boston: Little, Brown & Co.

CROUSE, RUSSEL. *Mr. Currier and Mr. Ives*. New York: Doubleday & Company, Inc.

DREPPERD, CARL. *Early American Prints.* New York: Appleton-Century-Crofts, Inc., 1930.

FORD, ALICE. *Pictorial Folk Art.* New York: Studio Publications, Inc.

FREEMAN, LARRY. *Historical Prints of American Cities.* Watkins Glen, New York: Century House.

LEE, RUTH WEBB. *A History of Valentines.* Framingham Centre, Massachusetts: Privately printed.

LICHTEN, FRANCES. *Folk Art of Rural Pennsylvania.* New York: Charles Scribner's Sons, 1946.

LIPMAN, JEAN. *American Primitive Painting.* New York: Oxford University Press.

PETERS, HARRY T. *Currier and Ives.* New York: Doubleday & Company, Inc., 1942.

Print Price Guide. Uniontown, Pennsylvania: E. G. Warman Publishing Co.

TOWNE, MORGAN. *Treasures in Truck and Trash.* New York: Doubleday & Company, Inc.

YATES, RAYMOND F., and MARGUERITE W. *Early American Crafts and Hobbies.* New York: Wilfred Funk, Inc.

ZIGROSSER, CARL. *Book of Fine Prints.* New York: Crown Publishers, Inc.

CHAPTER 15

BOWLES, ELLA SHANNON. *Homespun Handicrafts.* Philadelphia: J. B. Lippincott Co.

EARLE, ALICE MORSE. *Home Life in Colonial Days.* New York: The Macmillan Co., 1899.

HALL, ELIZABETH CALVERT. *Book of Handwoven Coverlets.* Boston: Little, Brown & Co., 1927; Springfield, Massachusetts: The Pond-Ekberg Company, 1941.

HARBESON, GEORGENE. *American Needlework.* New York: Coward-McCann, Inc., 1938.

KENT, WILLIAM WINTHROP. *Rare Hooked Rugs.* Springfield, Massachusetts: The Pond-Ekberg Company, 1941.

MOORE, N. HUDSON. *Lace Book.* Philadelphia: Frederick A. Stokes Company, 1904.

PETO, FLORENCE. *American Quilts and Coverlets.* New York: Chanticleer Press, Inc., 1949.

RIES, ESTELLE H. *American Rugs.* (American Arts Library) Cleveland: The World Publishing Company.

ROBERTSON, ELIZABETH WELLS. *American Quilts.* New York: Studio Publications, Inc., 1948.

WAUGH, ELIZABETH. *Collecting Hooked Rugs.* Watkins Glen, New York: Century House, 1927.

WEBSTER, MARIE D. *Quilts, Their Story and How to Make Them.* New York: Tudor Publishing Co.

YATES, RAYMOND F., and MARGUERITE W. *Early American Crafts and Hobbies.* New York: Wilfred Funk, Inc.

CHAPTER 16

COUSE, L. ERWINNA, and MAPLE, MARGUERITE. *Button Classics.* Chicago: Lightner Publishing Company, 1942.

DARLING, ADA. *Antique Jewelry.* Watkins Glen, New York: Century House.

GRAHAM, ELINOR. *Maine Charm String.* New York: The Macmillan Co., 1946.

LESTER, KATHERINE MORRIS, and OERKE, BESS VIOLA. *Accessories of Dress.* Peoria, Illinois: Manual Arts Press, 1940.

McCLINTON, KATHARINE MORRISON. *A Handbook of Popular Antiques.* New York: Random House.

CHAPTER 17

FAWCETT, CLARA H. *Paper Dolls.* Watkins Glen, New York: Century House.

FREEMAN, RUTH. *American Dolls.* Watkins Glen, New York: Century House.

———, and LARRY. *Cavalcade of Toys.* Watkins Glen, New York: Century House.

HERTZ, LOUIS. *Handbook of Old American Toys.* Wethersfield, Connecticut: Haber, 1947.

JACOBS, FLORA GILL. *A History of Doll Houses.* New York: Charles Scribner's Sons, 1953.

JOHL, JANET PAGTER. *The Fascinating Story of Dolls.* New York: H. L. Lindquist, 1941.

McCLINTON, KATHARINE MORRISON. *Antique Collecting for Everyone.* New York: McGraw-Hill Book Co.

MYER, JOHN D. *Handbook of Old Mechanical Banks.* Tyrone, Pennsylvania: Privately printed.

O'CONNELL, GEORGENE. *Miniaturia.* Chicago: Lightner Publishing Company.

CHAPTER 18

BURGESS, FRED W. *Chats on Household Curios.* Philadelphia: Frederick A. Stokes Company, 1914.

BURROUGHS, P. H. *Southern Antiques.* Richmond, Virginia: Garrett & Massie, Inc., 1931.

Buying at Auction. Chicago: Lightner Publishing Company.

DREPPERD, CARL. *Primer of American Antiques.* New York: Doubleday & Company, Inc.

ROBIE, VIRGINIA H. *Quest of the Quaint.* Boston: Little, Brown & Co., 1916.

SHACKLETON, ROBERT, and ELIZABETH. *The Book of Antiques.* Philadelphia: The Penn Publishing Co., 1938.

SINGLETON, ESTHER. *The Collecting of Antiques.* New York: The Macmillan Co.

WINCHESTER, ALICE. *How to Know American Antiques.* (Mentor Books) New York: New American Library of World Literature, Inc.

CHAPTER 19

American Home Pattern Book. Forest Hills, New York: American Home Building.

GROTZ, GEORGE. *From Gunk to Glow.* Deep River, Connecticut: Privately printed.

HALL, PEG. *Early American Decorating Patterns.* M. Barrows & Co., Inc., 1951.

ORMSBEE, THOMAS H. *Care and Repair of Antiques.* Robert M. McBride Co., Inc., 1949.

TAYLOR, HENRY R. *Knowing, Collecting and Restoring Early American Furniture:* Philadelphia: J. B. Lippincott Co.

YATES, RAYMOND F. *How to Restore Antiques.* New York: Harper & Brothers.

————. *How to Restore China, Bric-a-Brac and Small Antiques.* New York: Harper & Brothers, 1953.

CHAPTER 20

LEE, RUTH WEBB. *American Fakes and Reproductions.* Framingham Centre, Massachusetts: Privately printed.

ORMSBEE, THOMAS. *Care and Repair of Antiques.* New York: Robert M. McBride Co., Inc., 1949.

YATES, RAYMOND F. *Antique Fakes and Their Detection.* New York: Harper & Brothers.

The Things You Hear

DREPPERD, CARL. *First Reader for Antique Collectors.* New York: Doubleday & Company, Inc.

HARPER, GEORGE W. *Antique Collector's Guide and Reference Handbook.* New York: Harper & Brothers, 1939.

WHITTEMORE, EDWIN C. *The Pocket Antique Dictionary.* Marrimac, Massachusetts: The Rockbridge Co.

INDEX

Page numbers in italics refer to illustrations.